PRAISE
BECOMING A LEGACY LEADER

"*Becoming a Legacy Leader* is a treasure trove of practical expertise for aspiring managers! Get ready to embark on an extraordinary journey of personal development that unlocks transformative mindset shifts and a powerful leadership framework. Written by an accomplished manager and team leader, this remarkable book overflows with invaluable strategies for risk management, team synergy, influential leadership, and motivational prowess. If you want the winning mindset and tools to conquer any career hurdle, read this book!"

— **Susan Friedmann**, CSP, International Bestselling Author of *Riches in Niches: How to Make it BIG in a small Market*

"Zana Kenjar is a living testament to the transformative power of exceptional leadership. Her radiant positivity and genuine compassion set her apart as both a remarkable leader and an extraordinary human being. *Becoming a Legacy Leader* distills her vast wisdom into a valuable guide, giving you the sense that Zana herself is coaching you to leadership excellence."

— **Daniel J. Moreau**, President and Founder of For Love of Writers

"*Becoming a Legacy Leader* is an absolute must-read for anyone aspiring to develop and grow as a leader. This book brilliantly emphasizes the importance of building a strong mindset, becoming a leader, and leading by example. It beautifully highlights the significance of caring for your team and taking responsibility for your personal development. I highly recommend this insightful and empowering guide to all aspiring leaders."

— **Shaun Matriss**, Lead Business Growth Strategy Consultant, Wells Fargo Bank

"I absolutely loved *Becoming a Legacy Leader*. As an immigrant to the United States, Zana Kenjar has a refreshing perspective and an attitude about leadership and work that bubbles over with positivity. Everything you need to become a leader and create a successful team is in these pages along with a huge dose of goodwill toward caring about and celebrating your team members. The chapter on how immigrants can help themselves succeed—also extremely valuable to anyone in the workplace who wants to help their immigrant coworkers—is alone worth ten times the price of this book. Don't miss this one!"

— **Tyler R. Tichelaar, PhD** and Award-Winning Author of *Narrow Lives* and *The Best Place*

"Zana Kenjar's *Becoming a Legacy Leader: A 10-Step Manager's Guide to Unlocking Limitless Opportunities* is an enthralling and transformative journey. The book offers a brilliant ten-step guide that takes readers from being managers to inspiring leaders, with practical insights from the author's personal experiences. Zana's dedication to her readers' success shines through as she shares valuable truths and solutions to common leadership challenges. This mentorship in a book is a powerful tool that emphasizes integrity, empathy, and authenticity, empowering readers to make a meaningful impact in their professional and personal lives. This book is an engaging and relatable must-read that provides aspiring leaders with the wisdom and guidance they need to leave a lasting legacy of influence and positive change."

— **Dr. Pamela George**, Educator Consultant and Professor, Cornerstone University, and Author of *Unleash Your Joy*

"*Becoming a Legacy Leader* is an absolute gem. Zana's brilliance shines through as she artfully shares a plethora of practical techniques to conquer real-life challenges in the business world. What sets this book apart is the profound space it carves out for introspection and contemplation. It demands to be devoured from cover to cover since each chapter unveils essential insights and strategies that are indispensable for any aspiring leader. Zana's thoughtful approach not only empowers readers with actionable knowledge but also encourages them to delve deep into their leadership potential. This book should be embraced wholeheartedly by any ambitious individual with aspirations of making a lasting impact as a corporate leader."

— **Yukti Kapoor Mehandiratta**, India's Leading Transformational Leadership Coach and the Founder and CEO of SBY Academy LLP

"*Becoming a Legacy Leader* is a must-read gem. The author shares brilliant ideas and steps on how to become a great leader. The journey Zana will take you through to unlock your potential and become 'that leader' is an amazing experience. She walks you through every step of the journey. Furthermore, she helps you create a better team and more leaders."

— **Besiana Mullalli**, Branch Manager II, Wells Fargo Bank

"Zana leads with excellence, authenticity, and a pureness of heart. I love how she specifically addresses self-leadership and the heart of an immigrant. I am not an immigrant, but I have a huge space in my heart for the struggles they face coming to a foreign land, especially those speaking a completely different language. Wherever you land: a new or emerging leader, immigrant or citizen, balanced lifestyle or silo-focused habits, self-leadership is at the core of your ability to grow and Zana shows you step-by-step how to do it. Hats off to this warm yet power-packed leadership book!"

— **Cynthia McQuade-Brinkman**, Founder and CEO, More God Movement

"I cannot say enough good things about this book! *Becoming a Legacy Leader* will have a huge impact and will take you and your business beyond the next level! The author is a shining example, through her boldness, courage, compassion, and wisdom, of what good mental health and wholeness will do for a person, and she covers steps in her book for how to get there! The last chapter is an inspiring bonus chapter on immigration."

— **Tracy Rohrer Irons**, Founder and CEO of Our Voices Creations and Author of *Your Untethered Voice*

"If you want to go to the next level in your journey of leadership, this is the book to read. *Becoming a Legacy Leader* is a must for anybody who wants to grow and go to the next level."

— **Israel Hernandez, DTM, CPC**, Keynote Speaker, Trainer, and Author of *Keep Moving Forward* and *Dynamite: Powerful Principles to Strengthen Your Team and Culture*

"Reading *Becoming a Legacy Leader* has been a transformative experience for me as a leader. This book goes beyond the conventional notions of leadership and delves into the essential aspects of connecting and building successful teams. It brilliantly captures the essence of leadership, not just as a managerial role but as a journey of growth, motivation, and inspiration."

— **Reena Parikh**, Associate Branch Manager, Wells Fargo Bank

"This book is a must-read for anyone early in their leadership journey. Many organizations prepare their people to manage processes, but fall short in teaching individuals to lead authentically. *Becoming a Legacy Leader* fills that gap by providing simple, practical steps, clear examples, and a strategy of self-reflection. Zana Kenjar has delivered an effective tool for managers to truly transform into leaders. This book is designed to provide theory, practical examples, and ways to elevate a leader's impact through relationships and people-centered behaviors. Let's go!"

— **Donna Herbel**, Founder and Chief Igniter of Blue Phoenix Learning

BECOMING

A 10-STEP MANAGER'S GUIDE TO

A LEGACY

UNLOCKING LIMITLESS OPPORTUNITIES

LEADER

ZANA KENJAR

Becoming a Legacy Leader:
A 10-Step Manager's Guide to Unlocking Limitless Opportunities

Aviva Publishing
Lake Placid, NY
(518) 523-1320
www.AvivaPubs.com

Copyright © 2023 by Zana Kenjar

All rights reserved, including the right to reproduce this book or any portion thereof in any form whatsoever. For more information, address:

Zana Kenjar
zana.kenjar@gmail.com
www.ZanaKenjar.com
www.BecomingALegacyLeader.com

Every attempt has been made to source all quotes properly.

For additional copies or bulk purchases visit:

www.BecomingALegacyLeader.com

Editors: Tyler Tichelaar and Larry Alexander, Superior Book Productions
Publishing Coach: Christine Gail
Cover Design and Interior Layout: Fusion Creative Works, fusioncw.com
Author Photo: Bora Images

Library of Congress Control Number: 2023922233

Paperback ISBN: 978-1-63618-284-1
Ebook ISBN: 978-1-63618-285-8

10 9 8 7 6 5 4 3 2 1

First Edition, 2023

Printed in the United States of America

DEDICATION

First, I dedicate this book to the love of my life, my only son, Sammy Kenjar, and his future children and grandchildren. I pray he grows up to be the kind of compassionate leader who puts others first and gives without expecting anything in return beyond God's blessings.

Second, I dedicate this book to you, the manager who wants to become a true leader, leave a positive mark on this world, and create an everlasting change for humanity.

CONTENTS

Introduction	11
Chapter 1: Learning the Power of the Legacy Leader	17
Chapter 2: Step 1 - Building Your Champion Mindset	37
Chapter 3: Step 2 - Building Your Winning Team	53
Chapter 4: Step 3 - Fostering Diversity and Inclusion	67
Chapter 5: Step 4 - Leading with Influence	77
Chapter 6: Step 5 - Leading Your Teams Through Change	87
Chapter 7: Step 6 - Becoming a Customer Experience Expert	99
Chapter 8: Step 7 - Developing a Risk-Management Culture	111
Chapter 9: Step 8 - Becoming a Profit-Driven Leader	121
Chapter 10: Step 9 - Becoming Responsible for Your Own Development	129
Chapter 11: Step 10 - Leaders Create Future Leaders	139
Chapter 12: Bonus Chapter Accelerating Integration for Immigrant Success	151
A Final Note	175
Acknowledgments	179
References	181
About the Author	185
Hire Zana Kanjar to Speak or Teach at Your Next Event	187
Purchase Bulk Copies of *Becoming a Legacy Leader*	189
Enhancing the Immigrant Experience	191

"The courage to be vulnerable is not about winning or losing. It's about the courage to show up when you can't predict or control the outcome."

— Brené Brown

INTRODUCTION

"Success is not the key to happiness. Happiness is the key to success. If you love what you are doing, you will be successful."

— Albert Schweitzer

Many managers want to be promoted to the next leadership position, but they wait years for it to happen. They feel stuck, working year after year, but they do not help themselves get promoted to the position they want. Some have excuses, blaming the company or their leader for keeping them in the same role. In this book, I will show that moving up the ladder doesn't have to be that challenging; you don't have to wait for someone to dictate your future. That leadership job is within your reach. Just look inside yourself, and with my help, we will uncover your potential for becoming the leader you always wanted to be. Start today and take charge of your own development. Change needs to happen, and you need to be that change.

After finishing my degree in management science, I began my career as a manager in 1996, and I have led teams ever since. I have managed many diverse teams with different dynamics and of different sizes. I have worked hard to build a strong foundation and help pave the road to success for all my employees. It didn't start out that way, though.

In the beginning, I was the employee who took on more projects, the one who volunteered, and the one who was a backup for my own leaders. I trusted that those leaders would see my hard work and give me my dream leadership job.

So, I waited. And waited. I didn't have my voice and swallowed my opinions. And then a leadership role opened up and I applied for it! Much to my disappointment, the company brought in someone from a totally different state and gave him the position. I was happy for everyone but myself. However, even through my disappointment, I noticed what an amazing leader this man was. He was different. He genuinely cared not only about my career development but my personal development. He led with compassion and empathy, and he inspired everyone he came in contact with. He inspired me to look inside myself. That's when I realized it was not my leader's fault that I hadn't been promoted. It was my own. I was in charge of my personal development.

I realized if I had developed a better vision, believed in and loved myself more, been confident that I was enough, and taken the time to craft my own success, I would not have been forced to wait more than a decade for my dream job. I waited twelve years for my break, and after learning how to be a leader from my leader, I got the position! I was promoted over and over to higher ranks and larger teams. I was recognized as being in the top 2 percent of highest-performing managers in the country. I became known for my stellar customer experience and for turning around underperforming branches to make them overperform and thrive. I realized fear is what stops us, but fear is only a thought, and a thought can be changed. I want to change your negative thoughts into positive ones and thereby move you from a negative situation into a permanent positive one. It's never too late to change.

As typical with people who read personal development books, you might be asking, "How should I use this book? Should I jump around and just read the chapters I'm interested in? Are some chapters more important than others?" The answer is simple. This book should be read cover to cover. Skipping steps and cutting corners does not make great leaders. Read each chapter, do the exercises, and follow the instructions. Apply all the processes, strengthen the most important and relevant skills, and don't forget to celebrate your successes along the way. Each chapter gives you stories that will inspire you to do more and bring your team to greatness. This book is not just about your development; it discusses the most relevant topics and skills to the total lifecycle of your business and the overall success of your team. When you learn and apply this information and the accompanying tools, you will create a high-performing and cohesive team and be prepared for your next leadership job.

In the following chapters, we will recreate you as a legacy leader starting from the first component, personal development. We will see how to remove success blocks from the mind, body, and soul, and instill a champion mindset that will bring you to a healthier, happier, and more successful personal and professional life. Once you develop your routine and feel the peace and joy it brings, you will step into your office with the most valuable attire a leader can have—your smile. You can't take it off; you are incomplete without it.

We will dive into the foundation of building a leader, looking at risk management, and how everyone plays an equal part in our success. We will look at hiring and developing your team with character by learning how to develop a thriving, diverse, and cohesive team.

You will get valuable advice in the chapter about how to influence, inspire, innovate, and motivate your team and make them into high performers. You'll love the chapter about becoming a customer experience expert and will benefit from all the tools, resources, and efficiencies I will provide you and your team. With this information, your team will have expertise in satisfying the most valuable people in business, our customers, and with this focus, increased revenue is not far away. You will gain true success and learn to celebrate successes with your team daily. This book screams success for yourself, your teams, and your company.

Finally, you will learn the steps to becoming responsible for your own development and how to land the job you have always wanted. After you get your dream job, you will be developing leaders and multiplying the benefits of what you learn. The last chapter is a bonus chapter—it is about succeeding as an immigrant, something I have experienced personally, so I put a lot of heart into writing it. I have also included exercises throughout the book to help you reflect on and apply what you have learned.

I have crafted this book very carefully and included real-life examples of what success can truly feel like, both personally and professionally. It's a vision I wish someone had guided me toward in my early days of management. We are in this world today, but we might not be tomorrow, so get your gear and get ready to get to know you—the one who might have lost that spark inside and all the greatness in it, or the one who has the spark and wants to get there more efficiently. I will help you dig deep, uncover all your inner potential, and find your spark so you can shine forever. I am so excited for you to start this journey and to help you pave the road to success.

Let's go!

"Become a leader whom everyone will follow and leave a mark on this world by helping others, knowing the world will become a better place because of you."

— Zana Kenjar

CHAPTER 1

LEARNING THE POWER OF THE LEGACY LEADER

"Life is a dance, come and dance with me."
— Zana Kenjar

Meet Adriana. She wants to become a leader. She has been working in her company for many years, and she has been leading her team the same way for years. When changes and initiatives come, she resists and is not excited about the change, but she believes she deserves the next promotion. Whenever she interviews, she thinks, *This is going to be it.* But after a couple of dread-filled weeks, she receives the same email. "We are sorry to inform you the position went to a more qualified candidate." She wonders when it's going to her.

Are Adriana's interviewing skills rusty? Or does she need to change her mindset and welcome change with a smile? Who will she need to become to get the leadership job she wants?

_____

_____

_____

Dear manager, you may be in the same situation as Adriana and want to rise in the leadership ranks. You may have been working for a company for some time, or you may be a new manager hoping to accelerate the growth process and get to the top quicker. If so, this is a great book for you.

I wish I'd read this book a decade ago. Back then I had been a manager for a company for twelve years before I got my break and was promoted to a more meaningful leadership role. This book will give you a positive perspective and save you time in reaching your goal.

Come join me on this journey of transformation to become the catalyst of change, an unstoppable leader ready for a great challenge. Some of the processes I am suggesting are not new, but I have reprioritized them. And the book is not just a path to becoming the great leader you want to become—it goes well beyond that. It's a book to help you build a happy, prosperous life, a life full of joy and appreciation. I didn't have that when I was a manager. My life was a total rush, from morning to night, and ending with worries about the next day.

I want you to have the formula for a happy life and happy work and for developing a brand that will leave your mark on this world—a mark of your greatness! I know you have great desires, and I want you to feel your goals—the leadership position, the success, and the money you will hope to make—are within your reach, but you need to want the change, feel the change, and be the change. I will help you unleash the power within.

A great motivational speaker, Donna Herbal, told me, "If a person doesn't want to learn, they will be sad." It was a simple statement, yet so true. Let's not be sad. I am a very happy person, and I want to sprinkle happiness and great success on you.

> *"A leader is a behavior; when you change to a leader's behavior,*
> *you start pedaling in a world of joy!"*
> — Zana Kenjar

A true leader needs so many skills, competencies, character traits, and attributes. It's impossible to adopt them all, but in this chapter I will share the most important ones I have learned during my twenty-plus years in leadership. I believe they can help you leave an everlasting legacy.

COMMUNICATION

The most important skill to master is how you speak to yourself, your team, your manager, your peers, your business partners, your family, and the world.

Here is how to master communication as an effective future legacy leader:

Speak with sincerity and humility. Praise others for the great things they are doing. Maintain a humble attitude. Utter words with kindness. Let your heart speak the truth. Don't be afraid to recognize your limitations and be vulnerable when uncertain. Erase ego in your voice, and allow your true, authentic self to speak with passion and enthusiasm. Be respectful, and share information that matches your true beliefs and values. Furthermore, be consistent and understanding, and don't make promises you can't keep.

Carry influence in your voice. Learn how to tell stories and give examples that will persuade others to move to the positive side of the fence. Your voice needs to smile to capture your audience and get people to listen. Speaking with authority and using your title will not get you there. Wear a warm smile when communicating with anyone.

> *"We never know which lives we influence, when, or why."*
> — Stephen King

Display integrity and trust in your voice. To live in the world of leadership, you must have the utmost integrity at all times, and it needs to show in your voice. Recognize that this change requires total commitment to your company's mission, values, policies, procedures, ethics, and moral character. You can't deviate from this important element because you will need to teach your team and ensure they have integrity from the beginning. When speaking with integrity and getting used to doing things right from the start, you and your team are on the way to greatness. Remember, this is a fundamental part of your character, which you need to display no matter what you do. It will speak volumes of you and prepare you for great success as a leader.

Express empathy and compassion in your voice. Empathy is a great soft skill to learn and practice because when your team is struggling and comes to you, you need to put yourself in their situation. With compassion, you go farther in helping your team discover solutions. Many leaders stop at empathy, but I and a few others who display both have higher performers on our teams. Learn these soft skills and you will see a positive change. Think of yourself as a parent with two children—one child is empathy, who asks questions so they may put themselves in others' shoes, and the other is compassion, who goes beyond asking to helping others solve the problem. I have always done both. But if you just do one, it is okay—it's doing neither that is not okay.

> *"We all know the value and importance of being empathetic in our personal lives, but how often do we think about this as a key leadership trait? In our post-pandemic professional world, empathy is beginning to take center stage as more people and organizations recognize the importance of leading with empathy in this new era of work."*
>
> — Forbes

Let your voice reflect patience. Pause, listen, and reflect. When communicating, you must master listening. Speaking and listening go hand in hand because when you pause to ask a question, you need to listen carefully to the other person's perspectives and ideas to answer appropriately. It's important not to talk over others, interrupt them, or leave them feeling they were not fully heard. Practicing patience in your voice is not easy; it's a skill. It takes practice, like volunteering to speak in leadership meetings and partnering with others, mentoring and being mentored, etc.

Watch how you communicate nonverbally. Display exemplary nonverbal communication because it's important your body language matches your words. Your mind must talk to your body and ensure your verbal and physical messages are equal. Last week while shopping, I saw an angry manager talking to her team who were gathered at the register. I saw fear in the team's eyes. Looking at the manager's facial expression and body language, I was almost ready to pull her aside to give her some much-needed advice. Then she angrily walked away, stomping her feet. I have seen it over and over throughout my twenty-plus years in leadership. And leaders are still out there talking with authority but displaying nonverbal communication that undermines their message. Mistake.

Leaders must be aware of their body language and how it speaks to people. One day, I walked into the office and heard Sam, a team member, telling a coworker his manager had walked in with an angry face and headed straight to his office. Sam said, "It's not going to be a good day; he is in a mood." If as a leader your mood is down, negative, or full of low energy, it tells your team you are not the leader you need to be. Ensure you are smiling and that you are motivating, being eager to teach and collaborate. Respect your body and face. Display a sense of "I am here, happy and willing to teach you and help you every day!"

LEADING BY EXAMPLE

Leading by example is extremely important. There are many aspects to doing this successfully. Let's look at some of them now.

Empower and Develop Your Team. Empowering your team is a key skill, and as a leader, your job is to learn it. Working for your team and with your team is key. Empower them, offer them growth opportunities, and display your willingness to teach and lead by example. You will inspire them by showing them you are not afraid to perform any task, that nothing is beneath you. My fellow leader Melissa and I used to help our people clean the branches, and we ran errands before a big corporate visit or an audit. We helped our managers learn through roleplay with their teams over and over. We created easier learning methods; we told stories in our examples for team members who were struggling to learn to make the information more relatable. We broke down processes piece by piece, knowing everyone learns differently.

Overcommunicate. Overcommunicating was key, but we took care not to talk down to anyone because words can hurt, sometimes even more than physical pain. Words can undermine or reinforce someone's confidence and demotivate them even more readily than motivating them. When our team members succeeded, we succeeded. We were so happy when our people succeeded, which led to us succeeding. And it all came down to working hard to make it happen, to helping our people help us and themselves. When a team member told us of a devastating home or work situation, we displayed empathy and compassion as we listened carefully. We cried after, remembering we are human too and our highest calling is helping others. We were the most successful partners in the region because we were intentional about developing our people, listening, and treating them as we would want to be treated, which brings me to the next point.

Be intentional and clear. Become intentional and set clear goals and a clear vision so your team knows what is expected of them. Setting your intentions for the day, week, month, quarter, and year is essential. Thinking in terms of years is significant because you want to become a leader who leaves a mark year after year, helping a lot of people in the process. Set clear goals and have a clear vision of how you will get there. Set yourself up for success with intention, and intention's sibling, calendar management, which I will talk about in detail in the following chapters. Intention combined with calendar management is a super-successful duo!

Help your team problem-solve. As a leader, problem-solving is a critical part of your job because you are responsible for keeping the business running smoothly and problem free. Whether it be ensuring processes or procedures are followed correctly, resolving conflicts among your team, or handling customer complaints, you need to be well-versed in solving any problem that comes your way. Problem-solving is an essential skill you need to strengthen so you can address challenges within your team and your business to ensure the overall success of your office. Sometimes, you will have to solve problems under pressure, so you need to build resilience over time to get better and better at recognizing problems and solving them.

Stick to the communication skills we described above and don't compromise even in the worst situation. Solve the problem analytically by determining the root cause, its triggers, and its patterns. Be prepared to be adaptable in any situation that arises. Think on your feet, be innovative, and ensure you are always well informed about applicable technology and innovations. You need to respond quickly but responsibly in all situations, big or small. Prioritizing and managing your time effectively is key. Be able to identify critical issues, strategize solutions with team members, and locate and use resources to solve them. All these skills are crucial, especially in the risk management arena.

Problem-solving with your team requires a solid grasp of the big picture, strong relationship-building skills, and the ability to understand your team's perspective. In addition, understanding your diverse team's various worldviews requires you to continue learning and building on your skills. We will discuss this topic more in the following chapters.

Continuous communication about important existing and potential issues and solutions is an important ongoing best practice. To get better in this area, try brainstorming sessions with your team so you can plan for and stay on top of possible and recurring issues. When solving team conflicts, role-playing with your team, managers, and/or peers is a good way to find possible positive resolutions. You can also get help from a human resources advisor. Continuously develop your problem-solving skills and leverage resources like your leaders, mentors, and peers to help ensure problem-solving is one of your best skills.

Celebrate achievements with your team. Appreciate your team and each day's successes. No praise, no matter how small, goes unrecognized. Create a culture of recognition and appreciation. Foster an inclusive environment where everyone is successful and is praised for that success. Celebrate each milestone according to the team's preferences, cultural preferences, and personalities. Some celebratory activities may include handwritten thank-you cards, on-the-spot verbal recognition, monthly meeting recognition, organizing outings, holiday parties, etc. Make it exciting and meaningful, and ensure recognition and celebrations are timely.

Create Your Brand. Mary's story illustrates how to succeed so you get noticed in your company. Mary was a great leader with great passion for team development. She was an innovator who motivated her team and inspired them to be efficient and successful. She accepted change with a smile, always thinking change benefited her, her employees, and the company. She built relationships with her team and was determined to help them prepare for their next role. She listened to their perspectives and tried to incorporate their ideas. Her team was successful, and her numbers were above average. She was also responsible for her own development and was always looking for ways to improve her skills. She mentored peers and her managers, joined groups, volunteered for projects, and was always available to help others do the same. Everyone applauded Mary for being such a well-rounded manager. One day, a leadership position opened and Mary applied. She got the job based on all the wonderful things she was doing—Mary had built her own brand in the company.

Starting your legacy is starting your brand. Who are you? Are you your authentic self? How are you seen by your team, peers, and company leadership? My brand is being a leader in the business world who has empathy, compassion, and immense love for developing relationships with others. Then I can help bring them to the next level so they can have a better life for themselves and their families. In my personal life, my brand is thoughtful and loving. I strive to be a great daughter and sibling, a loving mom, wife, and friend.

I met the manager who gave me my leadership position at the beginning of my career. He hired me to manage one of his bank branches. A year later, I moved on to a different area, and he wasn't my manager anymore. But he watched me grow and prosper, becoming a great leader. When a leadership position opened, I applied. I had successfully turned a few underperforming branches around and I was ready. I was satisfied with the many people I had developed. It was time to help more people and on a larger scale. At my annual review, my leader told me I had an exceptional brand and he hadn't seen anyone as thoughtful as me—I displayed thoughtful acts to many, including my team, business partners, and peers. I am forever grateful for the success he helped me attain, and I will always be in his debt. He gave me the autonomy to lead, think like a leader, be innovative and creative, and bring my team to greatness through strategic thinking.

The moral of the story is: Build great relationships with others and trust the managers who truly see your knowledge, compassion, and skills and your ability and willingness to learn more. Ask for help creating and displaying your brand. Get a peer mentor so you can develop together and help each other along the way. Believe in yourself; be authentic, creative, innovative, strategic, and open-minded, and use new technology to help you become more efficient in the process. Your brand is ongoing and never ends. My brand will create a legacy, and it all started with my first manager, a decade ago, seeing my potential and bringing me into senior management. It's not about faith; it is about working hard and leaving a mark, a trail of success—people are watching. Most importantly, even if you leave a company, all your great deeds remain inside you. Life will give back what you put into it.

EXERCISE

Please answer the following questions to the best of your ability.

What is your brand?

_____
_____
_____

What have others said about you?

_____
_____
_____

What traits would you like to be known or remembered by?

_____
_____
_____

What influence would you like to have on others? How would you like to make them feel?

_____
_____
_____

How will you build your brand within your organization?

_____
_____
_____

How will you build your brand in your personal life?

_____
_____
_____

THE DIFFERENCE BETWEEN LEADERSHIP AND MANAGEMENT

Why is it so important to be a great leader? According to Gallup, managers influence at least 70 percent of an organization's employee engagement. That means more than half of employee successes or failures can be directly traced back to their manager. However, a leader is more than a manager. A manager tells people what to do and is responsible for tasks and processes. A leader takes the time to assess their team, motivates them, is innovative, and communicates with empathy. Leaders ignite the team's passion to do and be more—a manager tells the team which tasks need to be done.

A leader is humble, doesn't shout, is always kind and respectful, walks with pride, and wears a smile all day. By comparison, a manager can get stressed by the pressures of tasks and doesn't always communicate with empathy.

The leader listens, has patience, and develops a team member's vision consistently. The manager might become annoyed by slow progress and can be inconsistent.

A leader motivates others to do more and be more. A manager leans toward achieving specific goals or tasks.

EXERCISE

What does leadership mean to you?
_____
_____
_____

Who in your life has been a leader and who was a manager?
_____
_____
_____

How were these people different?
_____
_____
_____

THE VALUE OF PERSONAL DEVELOPMENT

Before I started with my personal development, I had never heard of the Calm app or learned about the many ways you can deescalate stress, overcome limiting beliefs, calm your mind, etc. *Why now?* I thought. How come no one told me in college? Or maybe I wasn't paying attention. I was still learning English. But what about while I was managing large department stores, buying offices, and working in a major bank? How could I miss these amazing techniques? I am a learner. You would think I would have stumbled on them at some point. It must have been the long hours I worked, six days a week, for almost two decades. I didn't have time for meditation, exercise, or healthy eating. Hey, I barely had lunch, and coffee was my friend. I even wrote and published two poems about coffee.

Yes, there are employee assistance programs, but what if we don't have the types of problems they help with? What if we need regular personal development courses to alleviate work stress and develop healthy habits? And what if companies continuously promoted personal development as part of your success solution? When I got into the personal development arena, I cleared all my limitations since birth and participated in every breakthrough session about self-love, success, relationships, and especially money.

After this discovery, I looked deep inside myself and found the true formula for my success, but first I had to identify and clear some limiting beliefs. As an immigrant and a woman, even though I made a healthy salary, I had a poverty mentality—I used to believe someone was going to take away what I had. I held on to money and always looked for sales in case one day the job went away, taking the money with it. I was in scarcity mode.

This fear was attached to how I grew up. My family didn't have much. But now I live a happy and prosperous life. I believe there is plenty of money to go around for everyone. I know this now, but I'll never get back those two decades living in scarcity mode.

I am telling you this so you can find what I found much sooner, especially if you are Generation Z or a Millennial. Know that you need total mind cleansing; you are not limited. Carrying old hurts, piled up one after another, is pointless. Thinking you are broken because of some event or a strict parent, etc. is a waste of mental energy.

You can succeed and have everything you want. You can have a champion mindset, an effective routine, and a happy face. I wish someone had told me I could let go of the things blocking my success.

EXERCISE

Now we're going to do an exercise about personal development so you can determine what you do well and where you need to improve in developing your leadership abilities. We'll do it in two parts.

PART 1

Answer first. Record your answer. Then ask a sibling, parent, or close friend to answer some of these questions about you and your communication style. Then compare answers.

Do I have an ego when speaking?

_____
_____
_____

Am I kind when I speak to people?

_____
_____
_____

Do I have triggers, and do I get annoyed easily with people?

_____
_____
_____

Do I always want to win an argument? Why or why not?

_____
_____
_____

Do I have any narcissistic traits? If so, how can I work on them?

_____
_____
_____

What does my body language say most of the time?

_____
_____
_____

Do I look happy and excited when I come and go from work?
_____
_____
_____

Do I praise or complain most of the time?
_____
_____
_____

Do I help my team when I communicate initiatives?
_____
_____
_____

Do I take the time with my team to ensure they understand the projects, and do I have follow-up meetings in place?
_____
_____
_____

Do I exhibit empathy and compassion at work?
_____
_____
_____

Am I a sincere and humble leader?
_____
_____
_____

Do I display integrity, and do I do the right thing when no one is watching?
_____
_____
_____

I hope you reflected on your answers and those of the person you chose. The answers were probably slightly different. How can you work to change any negative traits you identified?

PART 2

Now let's do Part 2 together. This exercise will help you find your "why," which will help you work on changing any negative habits in the following chapters.

Let's look at three managers who work for the same company. Their names are A, B, and C. Below is how they feel each day before, during, and after work. As you read about them, determine which one you most identify with.

Leader A—I am a happy and cheerful leader. I am always ready to start my day. I wake up happy, having had a great night's sleep. When I woke, I exercised and meditated or prayed. I repeated my affirmations, and I am excited and eager to start my day. I know it's going to be a successful day, and no matter what obstacles I and/or my team face, we will figure them out. I can't wait to put on the new suit I laid out last night—yay! I am going to look sharp. I wonder if my team will notice the suit and compliment me—especially Tom and Betty, who are the fashion police. While driving to work, I visualize a great and successful day. I can't wait to get to my office, greet everyone, and see how they are doing. I am prepared for my morning huddles and recognize yesterday's success, how Pat smiled and eagerly helped a customer, and oh, what a great handshake, and Pat didn't forget to walk the customer to the door. Pat didn't notice I was watching but will be proud when I tell everyone at the staff meeting. Pat loves being recognized for good work in front of everyone. I can't wait to see Pat's face!

Leader B—I wake up differently each day, depending on when I went to bed. I stay up late sometimes watching Netflix, and I wish I hadn't. Ugh, that's okay. Tomorrow will be better. I'll go to bed early and make up the sleep. I feel like I have no personal time—that's why I stay up. I wish my hours were better and I didn't feel so overworked. I will try to make it a good day. Our numbers are good, but I work long hours. I don't have time to meditate or exercise. I'll listen to affirmations in the car, figure out how to stick to my morning routine, and worry about it later. My team will help me get through the day. They did well yesterday. I am proud of them. Let me get my coffee. I may have to skip the morning meeting. It's okay to miss one day. I'll make it up tomorrow and share more success stories. Let's hope it's a great day. Oh, I love this coffee. I'm so glad I got it. It's waking me up.

Leader C—I wake up tired and wonder what the day will bring. I should start exercising, but I am not motivated. I work too much. I run to the coffeemaker and have just enough time to get ready and get out of the house. Sometimes I don't think about anything at all. I let my assistant do much of the work. I can't keep doing that all the time. I hope they don't say anything. I am happy I can count on them to update me on what happened yesterday because I had to get to my doctor for an annual check-up. I can't wait to have another cup of coffee. I don't know how long I am going to do this job. Maybe it's time to look for another. I hate this job—so much to do and they keep piling more and more on. When will it end? But I need the money. They pay me well, and I have a lot of vacation days I've accumulated over fifteen years. That's a long time. I haven't interviewed since I got this job. I am rusty. I can't even think about it. Let me stop for some breakfast.

Rate yourself on who you think you are most like—A, B, or C.

Here are some potential answers:

A—You are a great and happy leader; you are a leader with empathy and compassion. You love yourself, show discipline, lead by example, have fun at work, and have a balanced life.

B—You need structure: daily routine, dedication, self-improvement, skill building, and personal development. Start with a change and follow the principles in this book, and you can become leader A.

C—You need improvement in all areas. You need to improve yourself first, mind, body, and soul, and by practicing the principles in this book, with dedication and hard work you can get there. If you are not practicing self-development and self-love, you will not be able to teach, coach, and develop your team and model great behavior for them. You have this important job for a reason. Winging it and being miserable is not the answer. Your happiness is. Let the job go if it is not your fit.

Where do you want to be? I want to be an A for sure.

I conducted this survey with thirty professional leaders, and I can say 53 percent said they were between A and B. Others disliked their job. They all had one thing in common; they all wanted to be leader A. Many, no matter where they saw themselves, were unhappy at work and did not have much free time for their personal life. It's sad to say, but these thirty leaders were overworked and had no time for their families.

In my early days of management, I was mostly a B striving to become an A, but fell down to C at times due to life-changing events and not knowing how to get back up. But then I entered the self-development arena and learned to clear my head of trauma and stress. I am happy to report that for the past decade I have been an A, and it is a great life!

Once you become an A in your personal life, you will become an A in your professional life.

With twenty-plus years of experience in the business world, I have captured the true formula for success. No matter what you do, you must be resilient and access inner happiness to be successful. To really love others at home or at work, it is important to love yourself first. In this way, happiness can flow into everything you do. Yes, we need some specific skills to do our job, but we can learn those skills. Developing great morning routines, having a positive mindset, accessing internal happiness, and living in gratitude are the keys to success. With these tools, I believe you can achieve anything.

This discussion reminds me of a great book I read recently, *Unleash Your Rising* by professional keynote speaker, leadership strategist, and story breakthrough creative coach Christine Gail. She talks about how your intention and consciousness affect your decisions.

In her book is a chart called "Your Story of Intention," which outlines the different states of consciousness and how they affect our results.

In the disempowerment stage, feelings of unworthiness, shame, guilt, sadness, fear, yearning, anger, or pride can sabotage our decision-making process.

In the unleashing stage, we start to feel courage, gain confidence, surrender, let go, and have a higher understanding of what is needed to make the best decision.

In the reverence stage, we have compassion, gratitude, love, joy, and peace, and we are whole and complete. Our best decisions are made from these states.

I hope you enjoyed this chapter and learned you have so much power. Trust this book to give you all the tools you need for your current and next role. Now, let's dive into Chapter 2, Step 1, and learn about the champion mindset and releasing success blocks. Let's go! I am excited for you.

Before you go, check out the Becoming a Legacy Leader B.A.L.L Framework I created for you to serve as a roadmap for the ten steps you will be learning. I hope you like this visual, and let's start by turning the page. Yay!

B.A.L.L FRAMEWORK

"Champions aren't made in the gyms. Champions are made from something they have deep inside them—a desire, a dream, a vision. They have to have the skill and the will. But the will must be stronger than the skill."
— Muhammad Ali

CHAPTER 2

STEP 1 - BUILDING YOUR CHAMPION MINDSET

> *"The most important words you'll ever hear in your entire life are the words you say to yourself."*
> — Marisa Peer

The first step to becoming a compassionate leader and starting our legacy is to step into a personal development phase and create a champion mindset.

What is a champion mindset?

It starts with a belief. It is a strong, positive belief inside you that you are a great leader. Having a champion mindset means you are confident, and you believe you possess all the qualities and skills a great leader should have. You love your life and your job; you want to help your team and your company succeed; you are empathetic, caring, charismatic, funny, and witty; and you want to have fun along the way. Let's look at Jacob's champion mindset.

Jacob woke up energized at 5 a.m. and was eager to get on his treadmill. He blasted his music and enjoyed his run. He meditated for fifteen minutes and visualized the great day ahead. After a shower, he had his breakfast shake, dressed, and headed out. He went to work feeling his day was going to be amazingly successful and productive, and he couldn't wait to share what he had read about productivity with his team. He said, "It's possible for us to achieve great success. Our major ingredients are celebrating our differences, embracing challenges, and brainstorming new ideas, with everyone on board." His team was so excited!

> *"You are your only limitation."*
> — Zana Kenjar

How do you get to where Jacob is as a leader?

_____

_____

RECOGNIZE YOUR INSECURITIES AND LIMITATIONS, YOUR SUCCESS BLOCKERS

We all have insecurities. I had to work on mine one by one, silencing every negative voice in my head. I had to establish a champion in my head and groom her for the race I was about to run. I removed every hurt and fear I was holding on to from my head and reprogrammed my mind to release them. It's like anything else—things get clogged, and we need to clean them out and empty them.

As a child of eight, I considered myself an athlete. I trained in gymnastics and practiced every day, thinking I would go to the Olympics. I never got there, but I sure was in the game. It's okay to dream big. I had a great spirit as a child, and somewhere along the way, that confidence was taken away by events I was unaware of. Later, I realized how these events blocked me. It took decades to figure out what was wrong and how to fix it—and I lost out on a lot of fun.

One insecurity was implanted when my fourth-grade homeroom teacher asked us what we wanted to be when we grew up. Excited, I raised my hand and said, "I want to become a doctor and help people heal." My homeroom teacher, a tall, thin male with a dark complexion, raised his eyebrows and said, "With a mason father, you can't become a doctor." This block stayed with me all my life. It haunted me, and it did a lot of damage. This teacher separated me from my dreams and blocked my future before it began. It is wise to remember our words have power and to use them to build up and advance ourselves and others instead of tearing down and blocking people.

I had no one to talk to about this complex I felt. My mom was a homemaker, and my dad was always working abroad due to the economic situation in my country, North Macedonia. When my family came to America, I was just sixteen. The freedom I felt was all new to me, so it was a great change. I was ready to become a doctor, and my school supported me. However, I decided to take a different path. But it was my choice.

I tell this story to show that as many wounds as I had, I overcame them. I was raised to have a winning spirit, the champion mindset. I didn't let anyone take it away, and I want you to do the same.

EXERCISE

I have an exercise for you now—get your pencil and come back to do it. It will help you develop a champion mindset, I promise.

Let's start with some examples of people who didn't give up: Thomas Edison with his lightbulb filament, Sylvester Stallone with his *Rocky* script, Walt Disney being told by his editor he didn't have enough imagination, Stephen King's novel *Carrie* being rejected by thirty publishers—the list goes on and on.

Answer these questions by being very honest with yourself. Only you will see these answers—no one will judge you, so don't hide from the truth. Instead, start working on yourself right away.

Think about your insecurities, and when you are ready, answer the following questions:
1. What insecurities do you carry inside? Have you thought about them, or are you unaware of them?

_____

_____

2. How long have you carried them inside you?
_____
_____

3. What has hurt you the most? Are you still carrying that feeling?
_____
_____

4. Who are you? Do you know your identity? Are you comfortable within yourself?
_____
_____

5. Do you love yourself, or are you seeking love and approval from others?
_____
_____

6. How confident are you? Is it easy for you to deliver a speech at work in front of a room full of people?
_____
_____

7. What are your thoughts about money; do you think there is enough money to go around, and do you deserve to have an abundant and joyous life?
_____
_____

> *"A man must be big enough to admit his mistakes, smart enough to profit from them, and strong enough to correct them."*
> — John C. Maxwell

SIX STEPS TO RELEASING INSECURITIES AND LIMITATIONS

STEP ONE: ADOPT A DAILY ROUTINE

Similar to Jacob's story of adopting a daily routine, I want you to adopt your own. Everyone's daily routine is different, so start thinking about what yours is going to look like.

A daily routine gives you structure and discipline, and you will adopt healthy habits: exercise, prayer, meditation, visualization, affirmations, and feeding your body healthy foods and beverages before leaving your house.

My friend Bridget is a financial manager. She helps affluent people grow their money. Even with her responsibilities—she has two small children and a full work week, including two Saturdays per month—she still manages to exercise every day and loves to run in her local park. She also posts live stories on social media to motivate others. I love how she helps the world. Similarly, my friend Sabrina also has a job and three kids who participate in many activities, yet she manages to wake up early and run at her local reservoir, enjoying the scenic view and getting exercise. She looks amazing and a decade younger than she is.

Personally, I love my treadmill in the winter since I am always cold, but I run around my town in the spring and summer, and sometimes I take my bike to the park by my brother's house.

Research people's daily routines. Start with trial and error to see what works for you.

What does a daily routine consist of?

From the many motivational videos I watch, I have found many successful leaders have one thing in common—a set morning routine. I read on businessinsider.com that Apple CEO Tim Cooks has a morning routine that includes waking up super-early, 3:45 a.m., and exercising because the morning is free of distraction.

Exercise at least two to three times per week. It's amazing to start your day with exercise. It strengthens your body and keeps you healthy. I am not a doctor, but I have read that your circulation will improve and you will have more energy. I know for sure it's a healthier way to live.

To be your best in the office, you must have great energy and feel great inside. If you are not, it can break your morale and confidence. People notice when others exercise and take care of themselves, but the more important thing for you is to feel great! If you stick to it, in time, you will have the body you've always wanted.

STEP 2: DAILY PRAYER

> *"I pray before every meeting. It helps me stay calm and present."*
> — Jeff Weiner

Daily prayer has been practiced since the world was created. People from all religions of the world pray to God or their Higher Power, which fosters a sense of connection.

If you haven't prayed, or you are inconsistent, you can claim the power of prayer by simply talking to God and asking for whatever you want. If you want happiness, a great life, a career, and a family, and to have all your blocks removed, ask for those things. If you are feeling hurt, prayer can help you get back to a better state; simply asking for forgiveness, forgiving others for hurting you, and understanding you hurt them whether you realized it or not can provide great relief and peace.

> *"Have you any days of fasting and prayer?*
> *Storm the throne of grace and persevere therein,*
> *and mercy will come down."*
> — John Wesley

Get into a pure state of consciousness when you pray, and ask for forgiveness while letting go of all the hurt inside you. Ask your Higher Power to remove the hurt you embedded in yourself through misunderstandings, the hurt that is the most difficult to forgive. Maybe you have pain from long ago that is preventing you from moving forward. It could be a family situation that is hard to let go of and forgive. Those are the most painful. Release it by prayer, and seek healing in humility and honesty. You won't be judged, and if you believe pray will help, you will diminish whatever is preventing you from living a great life. Like the saying goes, let the past be gone and see what is in front of you.

Don't miss another day when you could feel better; time passes us by so fast. Make something great today. Ask for forgiveness and forgive everyone. If you can mend relationships with loved ones, even better. When they hurt you, they might not have known better. And they may need to do some forgiving themselves.

Look deep inside and make yourself whole to help build a better future. The mark of a great leader is humility, seeking truth, and wanting to help themselves and others every day. Pray with all your strength, cry, and release all insecurities and old pain. Ask for a better future filled with love, acceptance, and respect. It's there for you—just ask and start your happy days.

STEP 3: MEDITATE

> *"Meditation means dissolving the invisible walls that the unawareness has built."*
> — Sadhguru

A Mayo Clinic article, "Meditation: A Simple, Fast Way to Reduce Stress," says:

> When you meditate, you may clear away the information overload that builds up every day and contributes to your stress.

The emotional and physical benefits of meditation can include:

- Gaining a new perspective on stressful situations
- Building skills to manage your stress
- Increasing self-awareness
- Focusing on the present
- Reducing negative emotions
- Increasing imagination and creativity
- Increasing patience and tolerance
- Lowering resting heart rate
- Lowering resting blood pressure
- Improving sleep quality

Meditation has been around forever. When I meditate, I quiet my mind and listen to my thoughts for a while. If I have negative thoughts, I say, "These are not my thoughts," and let them go. This process is ongoing, and it should be for you as well. As you live your daily life, you will come across negative thoughts, and they will need an outlet. It's like reprogramming your mind.

To help you with the process, you could also listen to meditation recordings. One of my favorite meditations is the "6 Phase Meditation" by Vishen Lakhiani. It is about fifteen minutes—not too long for a morning routine and very powerful.

Other favorites of mine are those by Dr. Joe Dispenza, Marisa Peer, Louise Hay, and Abraham-Hicks. You should find your own. Listen to a few to see which work best for you.

STEP 4: VISUALIZATION

> *"Creative visualization is a powerful tool to help you overcome many barriers in life—in particular, healing."*
> — Vishen Lakhiani

Visualization is a powerful practice that can help you manifest what you want. Every day, visualize a great life ahead of you, a healthy body, the job you want, and the car you want to drive. Your thoughts can create your reality.

How do you visualize what you want to manifest?

- Find a quiet place.

- Focus on your breath, taking a few deep breaths and relaxing.

- Visualize what you want. For example, see yourself getting a promotion, buying your dream home, traveling to Rome, etc.

- Shift your visualization to a higher frequency and feel it. Use all your senses and make it very real, like you already have the promotion and everyone is clapping. You are decorating your dream house. You are in great shape and happy. Feel it like it has already happened.

- Hold the visualization for ten to fifteen minutes and repeat your visualizations until you see positive changes.

Before I bought my car, I visualized driving it. I saw my car in many commercials, and I saw me driving it on the highway. I saw it everywhere. I visualized it, and now I am driving the car I wanted.

Visualization has no limits. I do it often, sometimes weekly. It has become a part of my winning spirit, and it will become part of yours too.

STEP 5: AFFIRMATIONS

Affirmations are simply phrases you recite to yourself affirming something positive about yourself or your goals. Affirmations are like seeds in the soil. You say things repeatedly each day, and they become part of you—you program the ideas into your subconscious. You can write your own affirmations or listen to pre-recorded affirmations. You can create a positive belief in any area, depending on what you want to fix in your life. If you are struggling with achieving success, use affirmations about success, such as "I am a successful person. Success comes to me easily. Success is like a magnet for me. Whatever I do, I am successful."

If you want to maintain your great lifestyle, recite thank you affirmations: "I am thankful for this day. Thank you for my healthy body. Thank you for my prosperous life. Thank you for my joy." Add anything else you want to add.

You can listen to affirmations each day or write your own, which can include whatever you want to manifest.

I used to recite leadership affirmations before going to work by saying, "Today will be a very successful day for me and my teams. Today will be a fun day. Today I will only receive positive results. Today, my team will be successful," etc. Whatever you want to say, keep repeating it and make a habit of doing so. Experts say to recite affirmations daily for at least twenty-one days to get results.

STEP 6: LETTING GO OF NEGATIVE PATTERNS

Only you know your patterns. Think of the negative patterns you want to let go of that no longer serve you. Negative patterns can include seeing feedback as negative instead of something that benefits you and your growth. It can be as simple as not drinking enough water a day to stay hydrated or thinking negatively about yourself. Look inside to see what prevents you from becoming the best version of yourself and moving into the positive side of life—positive thinking is a healthy pattern for your mind, body, and soul.

SUMMARY

Let's now sum up the strategies for a champion mindset.

Have a winner's mindset. Imagine yourself as the winner. Envision the beautiful you standing up and receiving the trophy, or receiving the leadership position you always wanted.

Pass through the door of failure. Know that you must fail many times to get where you need to go—that's the mindset of a winner. Those failures are your strengths and the lights that will shine on you. I ask that you be kind to yourself and keep going.

Work on these activities. Develop a schedule of daily routines. Calm your mind and listen to your inner voice with meditation. Recite daily affirmations reminding yourself you are a winner. Visualize the winner in you, and release negative patterns. Imagine yourself as a leader who works for your people; is happy; treats everyone with respect; is sincere, empathetic, and compassionate; develops your team; generates revenue for the company; and wants the best for everyone, including yourself.

Act as a winner. Play the part and become the winner you are. Whatever comes your way, believe it will be a success in the end. Dress the part, look sharp, and have your morning rituals like winners do.

By training your mind daily, these techniques will become part of you.

Let's reflect with some questions. I included some samples of mine to help you with this exercise.

1. Have you ever wondered why the Universe allows you to exist?

Think about this for a moment—you have a higher purpose. Whether you are spiritual or not, everyone has a right to everything this world offers in our land of freedom. I love people, from poor to rich, and I feel the Universe put me on this planet to make a difference in people's lives and bring them to their greatness. I know this because I get the most pleasure out of watching people win, especially knowing I helped them become who they want to be and thrive. I have employed thousands of people, and I am happy to say I made a difference in someone's life, made their children's lives better, and helped a family live a happier and more prosperous life. Wow, that brings tears to my eyes and so much joy to my life just writing it and thinking about the people I've been allowed to help. (That's why leaders create leaders, which we will cover in the last chapter.) This is my champion mindset and what makes me tick. Now write yours.

_____
_____
_____

2. What are your strengths and weaknesses? What were you put on earth to achieve and be great at?

_____
_____
_____

I didn't know all my strengths until people pointed them out to me. Reflect on this question for a few days because it is extremely important to ask a family member or dear friend, especially about weaknesses. My sister-in-law told me my weakness was lack of self-love because I was doing too much. I was surprised at first, but I started working on loving myself more and listening to self-meditations and affirmations from my favorite Louise Hay work. Her work can be found on YouTube, including great free audiobooks like *Heal Your Life*. Hay is soft-spoken, and I share her thoughts with the people who need them.

Here are some more questions to reflect on.

Am I positive or negative at work most of the day?

_____
_____
_____

Do some things trigger me?

_____
_____
_____

How do I act? Do I practice empathy?

_____
_____
_____

Do I frown and stress all day?
_____
_____
_____

What are some fun facts about me?
_____
_____
_____

What do I fear most and want to get rid of?
_____
_____
_____

Take some time to think about your champion mindset. Answer and marinate on the questions for three days. You may find yourself thinking deeper and coming up with more answers, and that's when you will reach deep inside for answers. You can also add more questions on your own about the areas that are important to you.

When you reveal your answers, start working on releasing deep-seated pain, limiting beliefs, and negative thoughts—and start thinking like a champion.

> *"If your action creates a legacy that inspires others to dream more, learn more, do more, and become more, then you are an excellent leader."*
> — Dolly Parton

THE FOUNDATION FOR SELF-DISCOVERY

This chapter on self-discovery invites you to see where you stand with your personal development and how you feel each day. It is the foundation you will build your greatness on. You can bring your mind to a positive state in five minutes with a simple exercise. You have plenty of time to do this. I used to think I didn't have time for "extras." Working twenty-plus years in leadership and climbing the corporate ladder, I never thought I had time for myself. I would have learned how to pick myself up and bring my mind to greatness in just five minutes if I had known how to release the limitations I had held onto for decades, some since childhood. I would have told them to leave a long time ago. Bye. This is not your address anymore!

Then the pandemic happened. I was feeling overwhelmed like most of the country. I was scrolling through Facebook when I stumbled across an ad for a free virtual event. I was astonished by the things being covered—five days on how to be happy in every area of your life and so much more. I already knew those things, but I didn't know the names of the practices. I didn't know they had so much power. I asked myself, "Where have I been for the past two decades?" My answer was I was working and leading people to greatness. But if I had known this, if companies had offered these sessions, I would have become better, unstoppable. Well, I was glad I still had time as I embarked on a healthy life that gave me pleasure every day in my personal and professional life.

From that day on, I started investing in myself and many virtual events, including Tony Robbins' entire "Unleash the Power Within" (UPW) course, and I adopted these daily practices. I told many friends and family about them, and shared events on social media. Many people I know started the journey to a positive life with me. Many have been blessed with better lives and long-lasting relationships.

I also belong to many clubs and self-development communities where I have made valuable friendships and stayed in touch.

This chapter will help give you a roadmap to a happy life. First craft the truth of who you are and see if you have an opportunity to improve. Then start using some of these techniques. Or if you already started, maintain it and bring things into perspective for yourself. It is also a map to success at work. A happy mindset will produce great things. You will be a great leader. Your life will take you wherever you want to go.

In today's transformative times, now more than ever, you need to create a champion mindset. When you do, you will see a different world in front of you. You will be limitless in giving and receiving, in developing, laughing, and building the best relationships with your team. You will attract success to the person you have become; you will volunteer, speak on stage, laugh with coworkers, reach out to business partners, develop programs, love your personal life, find love, and strengthen family bonds. All this is possible if you just follow the advice in this powerful chapter and start down the road to personal development. You can release any success blocks—thoughts of being not good enough, not young enough, any fear of the unknown, fear of applying for a job, etc. No one should have negative feelings inside. Instead, they should have feelings of worth and abundance and positive thoughts affirming anything is possible.

Now let's start Chapter 3, where you build your winning team, and you get to create future leaders. Let's get started. I am so excited for your journey!

"Great things in business are never done by one person. They're done by a team of people."
— Steve Jobs

CHAPTER 3

STEP 2 - BUILDING YOUR WINNING TEAM

"Coming together is a beginning.
Keeping together is progress.
Working together is a success."
— Henry Ford

Now, imagine your happy world: You walk into your office and the atmosphere is buzzing with positivity and excitement. Your team members are collaborating, sharing ideas, and genuinely enjoying their work. They are not only meeting but exceeding their targets, and the organization is thriving. You are so proud of the team you hired.

This ideal work environment can be achieved through happy empathetic leadership. It is within your reach.

For me, hiring and employee development were the most important parts of my job. It made me happy when someone from my team got promoted and I had helped them get there. It brought me so much fulfillment when I contributed to making life better for my employees and their families. It brought magic to my heart each time. Getting the next person promoted was like an addiction because I loved seeing my team rise.

In this chapter, we'll look at the six key strategies for building a winning team.

STRATEGY 1: HIRE FOR CHARACTER

Behind every great leader, there is a winning team; behind every successful employee, there is a great leader. They take care of one another. Pay careful attention to this when building a team; you don't have to hire the most skilled people. Instead, hire people with great character.

How do you spot people with great character when interviewing? Here are the top seven traits exhibited by people with great character.

1. **Respect:** They treat everyone with the utmost respect regardless of background or status.
2. **Compassion:** They are kind and generous, consistently showing empathy.
3. **Honesty:** They communicate transparently.
4. **Responsibility:** They take responsibility.
5. **Humility:** They are modest and humble.
6. **Gratitude:** They give thanks each day for their team.
7. **Integrity:** They have strong moral character and do the right thing at all times.

How do you identify a candidate who has these personality traits?

The most important thing to remember when building your winning team is skills can be taught; it takes a little time and work, but you can roll up your sleeves and do it if you are willing to teach, coach, and encourage, over and over again if necessary. But first, you need to know if they are willing to learn and be coached—this takes character. How can you spot this character? Hard-working people succeed. Does their resume reflect success? People with great spirits smile while speaking and have great posture. People of good character shine with and ooze kindness.

My beloved father always told me, "Choose people with character, only those you would want sitting at your dinner table with your family." This advice guided me in choosing the right team, not just in my profession but also in my personal life.

Some of the people I hired for character had limited skills, some had no experience doing the job I hired them for, but they became part of our winning team, and I'm proud of them all. They all had one thing in common—their character reflected team spirit and love for the world. These individuals are leaders today with successful teams of their own, and they are welcome to sit at my dinner table as dear friends. Let me introduce you to a few of them.

LINDA

My first job after college was working as a department manager for a major department store. I hired Linda fresh out of high school. She was cheerful, funny, and a great communicator. I had faith she would succeed one day, and she did. Now she successfully manages a high-end cosmetic company. That was one of my first jobs, and even then, I had a general idea of what a productive worker looked like. When I left for the night, Linda took over the leadership duties. She would gather everyone and give them their restocking assignments, always checking their work for perfection. She used to say, "We want our customers to find their size tomorrow." She ensured team members helped each other so they could all leave together.

Linda and I go to restaurants together regularly or visit one another at home. I recently went to her mother's funeral, may God rest her soul. Like Linda, her mother Karen was one of the most amazing people God ever created. As a professional, Linda developed into a high performer before my eyes and learned many skills along the way, including her exceptional interpersonal skills. She is always welcome at my table.

REBECCA

I met Rebecca when she worked at the pharmacy I used. Each time I went to the pharmacy and purchased eye drops, Rebecca was waiting with a coupon. I didn't even know her, but she noticed I was always buying eye drops. They weren't even the pharmacy's coupons. She clipped them at home. This act showed me she was a woman with a beautiful heart. I recruited Rebecca to be a teller at the bank, and she was so grateful. She was a newcomer who was an accountant in her country, but she came to the United States with her two teenagers and needed to take the work she could get. When Rebecca started working for me, she didn't know the computer well, but we rolled up our sleeves, and together, my team and I patiently taught her, skill by skill.

Learning was not quite easy for Rebecca in this country, but after a while, she learned what she needed to know with our happy team embracing her and giving her resources and reassurance. She soon started to thrive. Repetition was key with Rebecca—she was among those you tell several times and then they get it. She reminded me of myself when I first came and cultural differences and technology were not a great mix for me. After a year as a teller, Rebecca became a banker, then a successful branch manager, and she was soon looking for her next leadership role. Her kids finished school; her daughter is a pharmacist, and her son is a doctor.

I would have Rebecca at my dinner table anytime—she is a trusted friend for life.

STEVEN

When I was managing a bank branch, I interviewed Steven. He had no banking experience, but during the interview, he talked about his success managing a fitness team and how he celebrated with all his employees when they met their goals. I saw he was an empathic leader and a star performer from his examples of caring, dedication, appreciation, and how he embraced everyone he worked with and the company. In my eyes, he was already a leader, but he didn't know it. After he came on board, he worked hard; he had a daily routine, calling people all day to get appointments. He cross-trained everyone, even the tellers, and his leads came from everyone. Our branch exceeded its goals with teamwork and a collaborative atmosphere where everyone worked toward the same goal.

Steven's development plan included becoming a manager, and I was there to help him work toward this goal. I tasked him with responsibilities daily, and he was quickly learning my job. Later, Steven took over my position and managed the branch. After successfully managing a couple of branches, he became district manager over ten branches. He is now an affluent business developer. I would have Steven at my dinner table with his family anytime; he is a trusted friend for life.

BRENDA

Brenda heard people in our branch brag about how happy we were and how we worked as one team, and she wanted to be part of that. She started as a teller elsewhere before trying to get into my branch. The first time she applied, I didn't hire her because I had a more qualified candidate who worked in our back office, and I had given her direct feedback for some time. The second time Brenda applied, she did fantastically in the interview. I hired her and had her team up with the service manager; Brenda learned her job and prepared for her next role. After some time, she became an assistant manager.

A promotion took me away from that branch. After some time, Brenda was ready for a manager position and applied for one in a branch I oversaw. She once again came under my supervision. I ensured she was great at executing strategy and managing risks effectively. She did this through empathy and by working side by side with her team. She was promoted to a bigger area where she managed bankers and financial advisors. She worked hard to get there; in the evenings, she went to school to finish her bachelor's degree and cared for her family, raising two children. In the end, her hard work and dedication paid off. I have occasional dinners and play dates with Brenda—she is a trusted friend. I would have Brenda at my family's table anytime, any day.

JERRY

Jerry was very driven; I found him at the last branch I managed. He wanted to become a banker overnight. He was a customer service representative who was very passionate about his work and very well organized. I set up an accelerated plan for Jerry and had him shadow me. He not only became a banker, but I soon sent him to get licensed—he studied day and night to pass his series seven license test. He was a hard worker and placed his trust in me. He was like my child; I couldn't let him down and gave him all the resources he needed, including one-on-one mentoring. Jerry became a successful banker and recently moved to another financial organization as a financial advisor.

When my younger brother was battling cancer, Jerry called me often and was always there to help. He advised me on how to handle the estate and helped me open all the necessary accounts. I would have Jerry at my dinner table anytime, any day; he is a trusted friend and a great guy.

> *"Leadership is not about being in charge.*
> *It's about taking care of those in your charge."*
> — Simon Sinek

STRATEGY 2: INSPIRE THEM TO GREATNESS

Once you have hired your team, it's time to develop and inspire them to greatness. The easiest formula to remember is to treat everyone like family and bring that same care to the workplace. This formula brought me a lot of success. Show your employees empathy and sincerity—free your soul of pretense, deceit, or hypocrisy. Communicate with respect, kindness, love, and empathy like you would communicate with your family.

Communicate with and develop your employees daily by using empathy and the loving, soft voice you would use to communicate with your family. I have seen many managers whose lack of communication skills frightened me. Some spoke down to their team, some used a high and unpleasant tone, and some sounded angry—that shouldn't be. Remember, you should embrace your blessings in having a team in the first place. Embrace them with positive, uplifting communication that will make their day and make them want to work for you.

Your team looks to you for proper inspiring communication so they can do better. I believe the way you communicate defines the quality of your work, your success, and your career. We all have different communication styles. Find one that works for you—one that does not rely on fear but is filled with respect and love for humanity, and shows your willingness to become the person your team needs you to be—their leader.

Inspire your team to greatness as you would inspire your family!

Always be genuine and don't be a different person at home than you are at work. Don't worry about your title. Remember, leaders work for their people. Be humble. Learn from your team. Recognize that you need development as much as they do. You owe it to your employees, and it's your duty to your company to inspire them, motivate them, and bring them to greatness. People who feel cared for perform at their highest level and trust you. Gaining their trust is a great milestone on your road to developing a winning team with members who continue to grow their careers.

When you care about your team's development with all your heart and do what is right for the team every day, there is no limit to what your team can do for you.

Good, simple, but not always exhibited examples of caring are bringing your positive and well-groomed self in early each day, wearing your smile all day, and asking your employees how they feel throughout the day. Ask them if they need help with a task. If their day was not very productive and they were down, show empathy. Bring them into your office and have a conversation. Never ignore anyone's feelings. It's your job to model and ensure the atmosphere is always happy and upbeat so everyone has a positive, safe, and thriving environment in which to work and grow.

STRATEGY 3: CELEBRATE YOUR EMPLOYEES AS YOU WOULD CELEBRATE YOUR FAMILY'S SUCCESS

Celebrating your team's successes, no matter how small, is very important in building overall success because success is built on small steps. When we celebrate success, it leads to much bigger successes later. Here you are highlighting the happy moments that lead to the proud moments. You want to start with small things—praise your employee for how they greeted the customer with a smile, made eye contact, and shook hands, and how they walked them to their desk and pulled out a chair for their customer. Make it count. Write a thank you note and share their success with the rest of the team in the next morning huddle.

The team learns to copy that behavior and receive the same shoutout. Recognizing small things leads to recognizing the big things when employees do a great job. Recognition will create healthy competition and bring positivity to your team. Bake a cake or buy a fruit salad and tell your employees you are celebrating going above and beyond in one category. If you did badly in all but one category, you can switch your negative narrative and celebrate what is working. What you are doing is celebrating what is working and avoiding being upset about the areas where you have an opportunity to do better. When you start celebrating things that are working and showing you appreciate what is great about your team, your team members will develop a positive mindset. Let go of what could have been and appreciate what is. Live for celebration moments with your team. Tell them, "We are going to be on fire and hit the rest of our goals," and start building their confidence. Say, "I am here with you. Let's learn from this and not carry regret over missed opportunities."

We can't watch yesterday's sunrise. Start fresh each day. Talk about what your team can work on moving forward, what they need to accomplish, and what bold action they can take. Don't overlook the small accomplishments—build on the momentum they bring.

STRATEGY 4: ENSURE EVERYONE IS SUCCESSFUL LIKE YOU WANT YOUR FAMILY TO BE SUCCESSFUL

As you know, your family is likely to have varying degrees of success. Some people need to work harder than others. Sometimes children in the same family can be very different. One may need to work hard to be better at school while another is very driven and school comes easy for them. Work with your employees one-on-one weekly to ensure they get the instruction they need to succeed. Help the ones who need more work and bring them to the finish line. At the same time, keep an eye on everyone, every day to ensure they are doing what they need to do daily because we are human, so our confidence can drop at times. You need to be there to instill and/or boost their confidence and lift them up.

STRATEGY 5: SHOW YOUR EMPLOYEES THE SAME EMPATHY YOU SHOW YOUR FAMILY

This isn't about mixing your business and personal lives. It's about bringing some of the care you show your family into your professional toolbox. Showing compassion and empathy by putting yourself in your team members' shoes is a great thing—and you actually win in the end. If your child is having a bad day, you would like to help them feel better, so you talk to them and try to understand what is wrong. By understanding what happened, as a parent you will know what to say or do to make them feel better.

Think of it that way when you are at work. Sometimes an employee will come to work and not be at their best and ready for the day. You don't know what they are going through or why they are in such a state. Never ignore such behavior. The best thing to do is have a conversation with them. Pull them aside and tell them you are there for them. Many will open up to you, even if it is a health or family issue. The most important thing is not to ignore the situation but address it immediately. They will feel so much better because their manager cares about them as humans and not just employees.

I had a situation where a high performer, Tracy, started coming in late and called in sick a few times. She was always upbeat, positive, and smiling, but she was unproductive. When I asked her if anything was bothering her, she didn't want to tell me at first. I told her, "Things happen but communication will lead to fixing problems, so tell me how I can help." Finally, she told me her car had been repossessed so she had to take the bus. I arranged a schedule change so she could come in an hour later—I aways had someone on my team who wanted to come in early. Tracy was forever grateful. Looking me in the eye, she said, "You have an amazing heart." I really wanted Tracy to have a better life. She was a single mom working very hard at juggling work and a baby. Yet with all that, she was a high performer and available for me anytime. I knew Tracy was a great banker, and when I saw a business banker position in another branch, as much as I loved working with Tracy, I wanted her to get to the next level and help more customers. She brought in many business customers by asking the right questions. In my heart, I wanted to help her the same way I would help a family member by bettering her financial situation. She needed the money for her child's daycare and getting her car situation settled, so I was glad to let her move up, even if it meant losing her in my branch.

This brings me to the next topic in creating your powerhouse team—do you give your team options, or do you micromanage them most of the time?

STRATEGY 6: PROVIDE OPTIONS FOR SUCCESS LIKE YOU WOULD CREATE OPTIONS FOR YOUR FAMILY

We can be very creative when it comes to helping our family. I am always looking for better ways to raise my seven-year-old son. I work to give him the space to think and tell me his thoughts, which helps us bond. I also stretch him to try unfamiliar things because his young mind is so creative. For example, I had him create a character he would love and write me a story about the character. He picked a carrot—he loves carrots—and named his character "Sammy the Singing Carrot." With some encouragement, he came up with a sweet story about the singing carrot. I asked him if he would like the story to become a children's book so all the children could read his beautiful, inspiring story of adventure and friendship. His face lit up, and he said, "Yes, Mom, and we can create a toy and coloring book."

I share this to show how we stretch our family to become successful. Do we do the same with our team? Are we creative enough to unleash their passion, their talent, and move them to the next step? Do our employees have options for getting to the next level of success? Many managers I have seen do not provide options for their teams or even themselves, and that saddens me.

I love the United States of America. It's the best country in the world because it is full of opportunities, and I will continue to create opportunities for myself, my family, and my employees until my dying day. Get to know your team, create endless opportunities, help them find options, and there will be no limit to who and what you and your people can become. If people have thriving mental fitness they can become whoever they want to be. As a creative and unstoppable leader with empathy for others, if you create a healthy approach to your team like you would your family, you will build so much confidence within your team. It's a great place to be and results in growing your business. Learn to apply these steps and set yourself, your team, and your company up for success.

GROWING YOUR COMPANY'S BOTTOM LINE

I know you will succeed if you lead with care for everyone, working for their success and celebrating their smallest and biggest successes. Some may disagree, saying, "This is too much to do—it's only my work; they are not my family. In the end, they will move on, and I won't see them again. My family is forever." That might be true for some but not all. I can reassure you that deep inside, everyone wants to be loved and be successful at work, even if they love the role they are in and have no desire to move up.

Caring is a formula for success—you give, care, and help your team; you give them opportunities and options for development, and you build their confidence so they thrive. Positive results will follow. You will be successful each month, and this will bring you happiness and joy in your heart because you are doing more than producing revenue—you are producing revenue collectively with a team filled with love, compassion, and care for others, family or not.

I call it love for the world. I love helping people build a better life for themselves and their families. By thinking this way, you will manifest a successful life for yourself. In Croatia, a saying goes, "The hand that gives is better than the one that receives."

EXERCISE

1. How would I want someone to treat my family at work?
   _____
   _____

2. What type of person do I need to become to bring my care from home to my team to become successful?
   _____
   _____

3. What do I need to do to learn to gain the emotional intelligence to help my team?
   _____
   _____

4. What difference can I make in someone's life? How can I bring them closer to their dreams, the same way I want someone to do for my family?
   _____
   _____

Building your team can be fun and exciting. If you have an existing team, work on the characteristics they are missing. Offer one on ones with consistent coaching, education, and follow-through. The world is full of beautiful people. Develop successful relationships, embrace people's diversity, and celebrate inclusiveness. Give love to everyone, and you will receive success and your pot of gold at the end of your journey. You will continue to grow along your path, leading larger teams with the same positive mindset and compassion that earned you each new role.

Now that you have your willing team, let's continue your journey of developing as a legacy leader by fostering diversity and inclusion in a workplace.

"Diversity: the art of thinking independently together."
— Malcolm Forbes

CHAPTER 4

STEP 3 - FOSTERING DIVERSITY AND INCLUSION

"In diversity, there is beauty and there is strength."
— Maya Angelou

Now that you have hired your team by focusing on their character and adopted the necessary skills and principles to inspire them, you need to step into the world of diversity and inclusion to ensure your team thrives. In this world, you will expand your mind, sharpen your skills, and build your legacy as a person and a leader. Furthermore, by bringing everyone together as one cohesive team, combining their unique talents and backgrounds, everyone will perform at their best for a common goal, a thriving business.

I was so afraid of all the different people around me when I first came to the United States. Being from Southeast Europe, I had never seen an Asian, an African American, etc.—only white people. I started my sophomore year in high school, and I had a ten-minute walk home. One day, an African American boy in my class caught up to me and said, "Can I walk with you? Where do you live?" I didn't know what to say, but I started to walk faster and faster, as though he had bad intentions, and didn't answer him. I was afraid of the unknown. He was the first African American boy to speak to me. To this day, I think about it and ask for forgiveness because I must have hurt his feelings. Maybe he knew I was new and wanted to be my friend.

Today, my circle of friends is very diverse. I met Jamez, an African American, when we worked together. We shared a love for writing. We wrote our first book together with our book coach. We clicked; I wanted her to succeed as much as she wanted me to. We share a priceless bond and experiences. I go to Florida to see her and her beautiful family. She completes me as a friend. She was there at the hardest time of my life when my brother was battling cancer. I was writing a book about that when I met her. She called me every day to fill me with positivity, hope, and grace. It's a gift of beautiful friendship, and I love her with all my heart.

BUILDING STRONG, DIVERSE TEAMS FOR A THRIVING BUSINESS

If you want to become a great leader, you must know how to harness your diverse team's potential. First, understand that strength and power lie in "diversity." Like the popular saying, "Diversity is the spice of life." The world is a melting pot of differences, and you must strive to get there, be there, and continue to learn and grow each day. First, be open-minded and get rid of all your biases. Believe each person is an individual, no matter where they came from. They had a life that may have been different than yours, with a different upbringing, culture, thoughts, and opinions. Embrace all the differences and start fresh. You already know to have a champion mindset (see Chapter 2). Work on yourself first. Whether you are a new manager or not, you must let go of any limiting thoughts and accept people as individuals with everything they come with as the true treasure they are. Trust that their worldviews matter.

ONGOING DIVERSITY AND INCLUSION EDUCATION

You have created an awesome team with people from all over the world. What do you do now? How do you ask questions without getting too personal? How can you learn the potential of each person and what they can bring to the table? Here are some helpful activities:

- **Take diversity training:** Ensure you take any training your company offers and learn the material, reading it over and over again. My last company was big on DEIB (diversity, equity, inclusion, and belonging). The education was ongoing, and you had to pass the courses. Sometimes you go through a course fast, then slow down to note the important elements to have them in your daily folder. Take some time to educate yourself about different countries, their culture, customs, cuisine, landmarks, and their beauty. Don't focus on political aspects—if someone wants to talk about politics, just listen politely.

- **Work with peers from different backgrounds and talk to your leader:** Ask questions, be curious, and extend a lunch invitation to a peer with an amazing, high-performing, diverse team. Join your DEIB chapter at work. You will meet and learn a lot about people, and it's full of lessons, fun activities, and international gathering parties.

- **Join diverse groups on social media:** I like cooking channels with the different food types and travel groups best. You learn how to cook new foods and find places you want to visit. LinkedIn is a great place to find discussion groups, and joining their weekly or monthly zooms is worthwhile. Also, you can create your own groups on your topic of interest. Mine are exploring travel, LinkedIn leadership group, and poetry corner.

- **Create diverse relationships outside of work:** When you are out and about, meet people and engage in conversation. Supermarkets are great places, as are restaurants, parks, and picnic areas. If you have kids, become a class parent, join the PTO (parent teacher organization) where you meet parents with different backgrounds, or get involved with the Boy or Girl Scouts, which open doors to activities and meeting people.

- **Volunteer for different projects within different cultures:** Volunteer for your favorite cause and meet people from different backgrounds who support the same cause. This will make you feel as though you belong to something bigger while you give back to the community. One of my peers was volunteering at a mosque and she needed volunteers to cook for the month of Ramadan. I had an amazing time helping, learning how to make different foods, and feeding people who came to the mosque to break their fast.

- **Travel to different lands and experience their beauty:** I have met a lot of managers who have not explored the beauty of the world. People who say they are Italian should explore the land of their ancestors to help them feel like they are Italian. I read that the most well-rounded people are well-traveled. I dare you, on your next vacation, to travel the world and feel the difference when you come back. You will be refreshed; your worries will fade away, and you can get to work with ease.

- **Experience different restaurants and taste the different cuisines:** Explore foods from all different lands. Don't be afraid because there are lots of healthy foods and preparation methods in many cuisines, and you will wonder why you waited so long. Food is special, and if you remain limited to certain kinds, you won't know what other cultures offer and how it can nourish your body.

- **Go to international parties and see how others enjoy life:** You are never too young or too old to go to a party—maybe the dancing isn't your style, but you can enjoy a beverage and mingle. If you get invited to parties, go and explore, and open your mind to different ways to live. Often, when I ask my cousins who were born in the United States to join me at a Turkish party, Albanian party, Croatian concert, folk dancing, etc., they refuse, saying it's not their thing. I used to love invitations from a couple of my friends who worked for the United Nations in Manhattan. I met great people there, including high-ranking officials.

BUILDING YOUR INCLUSIVE, DIVERSE TEAMS

> *"A diverse mix of voices leads to better discussions, decisions, and outcomes for everyone."*
> — Sundar Pichai

STEP 3 - FOSTERING DIVERSITY AND INCLUSION

Here are some great tips for building inclusive and diverse teams:

- **Building relationships.** Start building relationships at work with individuals. Notice how your team interacts as a group, and use your observations to make them a cohesive team. Take a forward step each day in your coaching and one-on-one sessions to learn one or two things about each person. Have a list of diversity talking points so you can pick up where you left off in the previous session and keep building on that relationship. Think about what is unique about this person and how you can harness all the goodness they possess and bring it to life to help them become the best version of themselves, free of prejudice, malice, bias, etc. Let the person talk and listen actively. Listening is the best skill you can have, and if you have opportunities to listen and interrupt, work on this skill. Building a relationship requires listening skills.

- **Believe in yourself and your team.** Believe you have created the masterpiece of a brilliant team. Imagine everyone interacting—your office is happy, there is laughter and joy in just being a team, and no one is afraid to share their uniqueness and the qualities they possess. Everyone is included. Customers walking in are fine with seeing anyone available, and there is no awkwardness where customers are waiting to see someone in particular. Don't let anyone walk away. You want an atmosphere where no customer has to come back later. Yes, customers can work with certain people, but you want the atmosphere where everyone gives top-notch service and has the knowledge to help your customers and put smiles on their faces. You can create this type of team. Believe!

- **Mix up your team.** For your team to grow, it's important to have many activities that help the team learn to work together. Call it a partner day. Mix up your team, and let them learn about each other, their work styles, and their backgrounds. Keep doing this so everyone has a fair chance to get to know everyone else. This will also cross-train your team for different positions.

- **Develop and monitor progress.** Ensure continuing education sessions are available and your team completes diversity and inclusion training and remains current. Develop team members in the areas you think they need help. Suggest all the activities you are doing or have done so they can become very familiar with this topic.

- **Be aware of unconscious bias.** Communicate the importance of understanding unconscious biases with your team and develop a clear picture of how they interact in every situation. Have an exercise in your meetings where they write for ten minutes about their unconscious biases. Let them reflect on what they wrote and have them write an action statement to address and learn about their bias. In addition, in your regularly scheduled one-on-one talks with them about their progress, ensure they are still moving in the same direction. Innovate and motivate them, and show them a vision of what that would look like. Provide them with resources and set milestones. Celebrate their success with a recognition email, ecard, or handwritten postcard.

- **Give praise, positive feedback, and appreciation.** When observing your team, look for ways of celebrating cultural differences and give positive feedback when you see diversity being celebrated. Recognition goes a long way; your team will be learning a lot when you practice recognition daily. If a customer is talking to one of your team members about traveling to a different country, and the team member is engaging and building a relationship, recognize their efforts. Love of travel helps people bond, and it strengthens the relationship with the customer, which encourages them to come back to tell your team member more. This creates customer loyalty, especially when a team member is well-versed in various topics of interest. Appreciate your team for going above and beyond in embracing diversity. Celebrate it!

"When we listen and celebrate what is both common and different, we become wiser, more inclusive, and better as an organization."

— Pat Wadors

CREATE AN INCLUSIVE CULTURE WITH SHARED CELEBRATIONS

Celebrations create joy and happiness and bring people together. We have many celebrations at home, and families have created celebratory traditions of various types throughout history.

Organize celebration traditions and schedule them with your team. Some team celebrations you can create at work include:

Holiday Parties: Introduce holiday parties first because everyone is excited to mingle at a holiday party since it brings in the holiday spirit of fun and joy. Ensure you schedule holiday parties at the ends of shifts, during lunch, or you take it offsite to a restaurant, depending on team consensus and availability. For me, changing the atmosphere and having the holiday dinner outside creates relationship-building opportunities and brings the team together. You can also extend the invitation to bring a plus one if your company allows.

International Potluck: If you want to bring diversity and celebrate international foods, this tradition will make relationships closer since food is an essential element of gatherings. I believe many people love potlucks—everyone likes trying something different and exploring cultures through food. You can have this party twice a year or annually, depending on how many parties your team collaboratively decides to adopt as a tradition in your branch, office, etc.

Birthday Celebrations: Birthday celebrations are great and cannot be skipped unless team members are not celebrating their birthdays due to religious beliefs or other reasons. This is an individual preference, but you as a manager can send an ecard or bring a fruit salad for everyone to enjoy. It depends on what the employees' preference is.

Team Success Party: This is a special party to celebrate your team's success. Making it a tradition will provide incentive to team members who are not being recognized to do better. You can have this party quarterly to celebrate the successes of your team members regularly.

EXERCISE

1. Name three countries you'd like to visit and add a traveling date.
   _____
   _____
   _____

2. Name three people you would like to meet from different backgrounds.
   _____
   _____
   _____

3. Name three different cuisines you'd like to try, and add a date to make reservations by to taste their foods.
   _____
   _____
   _____

EXERCISES FOR YOUR TEAM

Add diversity brainstorming sessions to your team's monthly meetings and have each team member do a different diversity exercise to learn something new.

For example, when I joined Sal's monthly meeting, one member of his team gave us a handout on how to say hello in various languages, and asked us to circle the ones we knew. It was fun. Another researched a team member's country and asked us questions. I was not familiar with the country, but the exercise made me curious.

_____
_____
_____

Now let's jump into Chapter 5, the powerful topic of "influence" and the affect you have on others.

"Actions speak louder than words, and a smile says, 'I like you. You make me happy. I am glad to see you.' That is why dogs make such a hit. They are so glad to see us that they almost jump out of their skins. So, naturally, we are glad to see them."
— Dale Carnegie

CHAPTER 5

STEP 4 - LEADING WITH INFLUENCE

"Think twice before you speak because your words and influence will plant the seed of either success or failure in the mind of another."
— Napoleon Hill

Knowing how to influence is crucial to successful leadership. The best way to become a great leader is to become a person with positive influence so you can inspire your team to do the job effectively and with ease. You need the ability to inspire, motivate, and guide your team members toward achieving a common goal. What is your ability to influence? How do you develop the ability to influence? This chapter will answer all those questions, but first, let's have an example of what life looks like when you are able to influence.

Andrew's team was unstoppable, always going above and beyond. Projects were done before deadlines, and the team members were always collaborating, celebrating, and giving praise to each other. Everyone knew their strengths and sought help from each other. Andrew was behind his team with his ability to influence. He always had his sleeves rolled up to help them. He had time for everyone and respected their time, making sure everyone ate first, that he knew everyone's communication style, and that he showed he valued their unique perspectives. He got to know them beyond the office because they felt safe and shared their family lives, cultural beliefs, love for travel, and other personal information with him. Andrew inspired them and built a positive environment where everyone was heard. Wouldn't you love to have an office that thrives like Andrew's?

Of course you would. Following are seven simple actions for how you can become an influential leader with your team:

ACTION 1: BE YOURSELF AND LEAD BY EXAMPLE

One of the best ways to influence others is to totally be yourself and lead by example. Don't expect a new title to change who you are inside. Employees will see your actions. When they feel their leader is sincere and they see that leader provides them with the space to be themselves, they will open up. When you are a leader, everyone looks up to you for different reasons, so the very best way to influence them so you bring out the best in them is by example. Live by the same rules you set for your teammates. Let them see your willingness to help them get to their desired destination. Let them see you as a peaceful and cheerful leader who wants the best for them.

ACTION 2: BUILD TRUST THROUGH EFFECTIVE AND TIMELY COMMUNICATION

Communicate with the same tone at all times. Communicate with transparency, and communicate with empathy and compassion. Overcommunicate as needed to let your team know you care. Practice smiling when speaking. Practice your posture and facial expression by looking in a mirror to ensure they match your tone and words when you communicate. Good communication is vital to being a good leader. Lead and communicate with empathy and compassion, and always make sure your words match your actions and not otherwise. One thing my team has always loved about me is my timely and consistent communication. At times, perhaps I sounded like a broken record, but it was necessary to ensure everyone understood what was needed. It didn't bother me at all to repeat what I had communicated the day before or just a few hours earlier. I know people learn better when they know their leader cares, so I communicated with humor and promoted office fun. One thing I learned from my coach, Tony Robbins, is that a good leader is a good and effective communicator. To get better at your communications skills, work on your confidence, take classes and training, have a mentor, and practice in front of a mirror with a microphone.

That last part might sound humorous, but it worked for Jennifer, the manager of a department store chain. She would use a microphone in her morning meeting. She would put on a fun song and ask everyone to change their state of mind. She gave her morning meeting an energizing atmosphere by asking her team to think of an upbeat song, and then they would pass around the microphone and sing their upbeat songs. Fun, right? Tony Robbins calls this concept "changing your state," meaning changing your physiology, getting your body to move. I love it and live by this concept. Later on, Jennifer applied and was promoted to a learning and development consultant job. Super-nice, right? Furthermore, one of her direct reports was promoted to her position. He continued her legacy by conducting his meetings with a microphone.

To help yourself become a great speaker so you can communicate effectively, you can take a course in public speaking; be the first to give a speech at family gatherings or meetings; volunteer to speak at special programs and events; and encourage your team to do the same and practice with them. In meetings, ensure you have volunteers ready to speak. Doing the right thing at all times and not deviating from it builds trust in you as a great speaker. When you add leading with your heart, leading with empathy, and being compassionate to your communication skills, you have a great mix for gaining influence.

ACTION 3: DEVELOP POSITIVE RELATIONSHIPS

Developing a positive relationship with each team member is a great start to building influence. As time goes on, consistent coaching and one-on-one time will help you develop positive relationships with your team members. Before the meeting starts, it's very important to ask your team members how they are. Also, recall the conversation from last time and ask them about how things went that you discussed then. They might not share much at the beginning, but if you are consistent in asking the same question before you get to business, they will share more and more at each successive meeting. They will tell you about their kids, where they went for the weekend, etc. Knowing their preferences for how to be recognized is also important. Learning about their unique perspectives will give you insight on how to influence them. As time goes on, by nurturing your relationships with respect and a concern for what's in it for them, you will develop solid relationships of trust in which team members will automatically be influenced by you.

ACTION 4: SUPPORTING DEVELOPMENT THROUGH CARE

The leader's job is to develop team members so they are prepared to take the next step. The team member is responsible for their development and must do the assignments. The key to getting there is holding your team accountable. Make their one-on-ones count by ensuring they have their action items done, whether it is working on a specific skill, learning public speaking, working on their goals, or continuing education. When they see you supporting them and displaying consistency about their development, they will feel the care you have for them. Ensure you work with a timeline; communicate with your team member about when they will be ready for the next step, and show them what that step looks like. If a team member is not keeping up with the original timeline, find additional activities to help them get there, whether it is additional training, mentoring, or cross-trained teams, etc. Celebrate their milestones with their choice of recognition. They will put their trust in you because you inspire them to do better.

ACTION 5: BECOME RESILIENT

Empower and motivate your team with your influence and the picture you paint. They will feel safe with you and the safe environment you built. Take a step farther and challenge them to reach for the sky. Take them to a level they haven't been to because you see that place in them. Ensure they become champions of change and do better and better each day. When you see them going above and beyond, especially with something outside their job description, point it out and celebrate it. Tina was a teller I worked with. I saw so much power and passion in her for going above and beyond her duties to help her customers. She cared about and knew all her customers' names. One day, a customer named Anna called Tina to let her known she'd had her baby. Ha! I thought it was so beautiful that someone who had just given birth would be thinking about my team member. I was honored. Later, I invited Anna to bring the baby into the bank to surprise Tina. Unexpected gestures go a long way in solidifying your influence with your team.

ACTION 6: BE TRANSPARENT ABOUT TASKS AND THEIR EXECUTION

The worst thing you can do is assign a task without thoroughly explaining how to do it. I have seen it often. The manager is busy, has meetings, the office is full, and customers are calling—I get it; I have been there. I have also seen a lot of compliance issues being generated by letting team members figure out how to perform a task without clear instructions. Even with trusted employees, without thorough, transparent instructions, noncompliance issues can arise, which can have negative consequences. Give your team complete instructions with total transparency about tasks and processes, understand their knowledge and expertise, and be there for them step-by-step until they get the task right.

ACTION 7: BE PROACTIVE AND ASK FOR FEEDBACK FROM PEERS AND YOUR MANAGER

We all need feedback; I love getting feedback because when we are in our environment, we can't see what others see. Have a mentor, a peer, or your manager spend a few days in your office to gauge the influence you have and give you some pointers. If you are working remotely, they can join your conference calls. I did this because I know influence is the best resource you can have to bring your team to greatness. In the same way, you can peel the layers of your team members and bring out the warriors in them. The more you know about their passions, the more influence you will have.

EXERCISE

1. Have your leaders or peers said you are a great influencer? If so, how?

   _____
   _____

2. What inspires your team?

   _____
   _____

3. In what ways do you show you care about your team's development?

   _____
   _____

4. Are you consistent in developing your team? Where can you improve?

   _____
   _____

5. How do they want to be recognized?

   _____
   _____

6. Do you provide a safe space and a positive atmosphere? How can you improve?

   _____
   _____

7. Do you think your team feels heard and seen by you? If not, how can you change that?

   _____
   _____
   _____

STEP 4 - LEADING WITH INFLUENCE

8. What makes your team members smile?
_____
_____
_____

9. How can you build stronger relationships with each team member? Think about each one individually.
_____
_____
_____

10. Do you believe your team trusts you? Why?
_____
_____
_____

11. Do you give your team complete and accurate instructions for the tasks or processes they are required to perform/follow? Do you work with them to ensure they understand and do the task correctly?
_____
_____
_____

12. Who has the greatest influence on you?
_____
_____
_____

13. How can you increase your influence?
_____
_____
_____

"You can make more friends in two months by becoming interested in other people than you can in two years by trying to get other people interested in you."
— Dale Carnegie, *How to Win Friends and Influence People*

Influence goes a long way. One of my favorite books of all time—we were even assigned it in my leadership course—is Dale Carnegie's 1936 self-help book *How to Win Friends and Influence People*. With 30 million copies sold worldwide, it is one of the best-selling books of all time. Carnegie began conducting business education courses in New York City in 1912 and did so for many years. He writes, "Never begin by announcing, 'I am going to prove so-and-so to you.' That's bad. That's tantamount to saying: 'I am smarter than you are; I am going to tell you a thing or two and make you change your mind.'"

This advice resonated with me because I used to say that in my early days, but Carnegie taught me if you are going to prove anything, don't tell anyone; just do it subtly so no one feels you are putting them down.

In the next chapter, we will look at the fifth step in becoming a legacy leader, which is leading your team through change. Through coaching and developing your winning team by inspiring and motivating them, you can help them learn to accept and embrace change in the workplace. Let's be the change and bring change to others with greatness. Let's go!

"Slowness to change usually means fear of the new."
— Philip Crosby

CHAPTER 6

STEP 6 - LEADING YOUR TEAMS THROUGH CHANGE

"Successful leaders see the opportunities in every change, rather than the obstacles."
— John C. Maxwell

Samantha was a manager and a catalyst for change. Every time change came, she would bring a cake to work to celebrate with the team because she said, "Something innovative is coming; new technology will bring more efficiency." The team would eat the cake with some coffee at the meeting, and everything she talked about was positive. She separated her team into groups, and every group had to brainstorm an innovative strategy to implement the change using the goal-setting formula SMART (specific, measurable, attainable, relevant, and timely). The team was excited, which made the change easy and welcome. Everyone was on board.

How did Samantha create this culture? Dear reader, welcome to life—it's all about change. We start as babies and change continuously, even in the grave. Why do some people resist change? Change means things will be different. Our comfort zones aren't usually "different." Comfort seems to be the opposite of change. Some people are attached to the old, mostly because it is comfortable, even though the old might not be so great. As humans, we tend to get attached to things, processes, people, and ideas.

How you deal with change in your personal life is how you will deal with change in your professional life. It's your mindset. If you don't handle change well in your personal life, I don't believe you can switch mindsets that easily and say, "Now I am going to work, and I need my mindset to switch so I embrace change." As you know, we deal with change often in our personal life. Change happens daily as we deal with our household, our families, and our kids. Daily purchases and creating debt is a change. Buying a new car is a change. We change every year as we age—some see aging as a blessing, but some won't celebrate their birthdays. I believe the way you deal with change in your personal life is the most important area to work on. Analyze it. Marinate on it for a week to understand how you deal with change. Then work to develop positive beliefs when leading with change.

EXERCISE

1. Below are five negative personal reactions to change and five negative professional reactions. Where do you find yourself? Circle one or more, indicating where you are.

   Five possible reactions to change in your personal life:

   1. I am angry when it doesn't go my way.
   2. I am shocked and don't want to hear it.
   3. I disagree with the change.
   4. I am uneasy about the change.
   5. I am sad and shutting down.

   Five reactions to change in your professional life:

   1. I am shocked and can't believe it.
   2. Something new again—when is this going to stop?
   3. I am not doing it this way.
   4. I miss the old process, but I didn't care about it in the first place.
   5. I am uncomfortable and resent the change.

2. Do you have similar patterns in both? Why do you think you are resistant in this way?

_____
_____
_____

3. Now choose and circle the positive mindset that resonates with you.

   Five reactions to change in your personal life:

   1. Good, I can't wait to work on this.
   2. I will figure it out.
   3. It's life, and life does the unexpected.
   4. I get to shift things around.
   5. I will find a way; I always do.

   Five reactions to change in your professional life:

   1. I think this is good.
   2. We will find a solution as a team.
   3. Life is a change and we are in it.
   4. Let's welcome the change.
   5. I like finding solutions with a smile.

4. Do you have similar patterns in both? How did this exercise feel?

_____
_____
_____

Now, create your own positive patterns with your own reactions. Then do this exercise in a team meeting. Try to steer them to transform the negative from both personal and professional to positive thoughts. Remember, our thoughts create our reality, and to change our thoughts, we can introduce positive affirmations.

The negative mindset toward change.

5. What are five negative reactions to change in your personal life?

    1.

    2.

    3.

    4

    5.

6. What are five negative reactions to change in your professional life?

    1.

    2.

    3.

    4.

    5.

7. Now revise the negative reactions above into positive ones.

    Five positive reactions to change in your personal life:

    1.

    2.

    3.

    4

    5.

Five positive reactions to change in your professional life:

1.

2.

3.

4.

5.

8. Do you and your team have similar patterns in both? How did this exercise resonate with your team?

_____

_____

_____

When you create a positive person inside yourself by recognizing your patterns and changing them, no matter the circumstance, you can endure anything that comes your way.

Things to work on with your team when dealing with change in the workplace include your delivery, your transparency, and your positive attitude toward change. This has worked for many successful leaders in helping them build a positive, cohesive environment for their teams.

Change is needed in the workplace. As leaders, we need to make necessary changes to be more efficient, even if change is pushed on us like a heavy mountain and we are overwhelmed ourselves. Whatever the change, sometimes it is uncomfortable. We need to take it as it comes, and support our team.

All new strategies come with change. How are we going to push through the new and resolve the old process? Some might yearn for the old process and feel self-doubt, while others embrace the new and take action.

Some managers may say, "Team, I just came back from a meeting, and we have this new initiative. Leadership told us it has to get done. Here it is; it's not my idea, so don't blame me." I have seen managers avoid taking ownership of new initiatives and new ways of doing things, introducing the change to their teams as coming from higher up the ladder. This type of communication is detrimental to teams and creates a toxic atmosphere without trust in overall leadership. It's hard to thrive in such a negative atmosphere. If you resist, it's hard to teach your team about what's to come. Talk to your leader to improve through resources, mentorship, etc.

The best way is to accept and embrace change as it comes and own it as a manager, communicating as one team with the company, leadership, and your team.

When change comes, have collaborative brainstorming sessions, create a strategy to implement the change, and start working on it.

Some great leaders have said acceptance is the first step toward change, and it's easier to move forward and create lasting results. Let's start with acceptance first.

> *"The people who are crazy enough to think they can change the world are the ones who do."*
> — Steve Jobs

ACCEPTING THE CHANGE EARLY

Acceptance is key to growing and striving toward the future. Know that change can bring us lots of success. Be excited when presenting the change. Say, "This is our awesome new initiative." And welcome it with your team. Continue to think of the positive aspects and how they can improve the organization. Highlight the benefits of the change. Communicating effectively and keeping your team informed with a positive posture and body language is key to your presentation. Communication about the change should be constant—schedule it and ensure you keep your team involved. Be aware of challenges along the way and crush them with your innovative thinking, motivation, and inspiration.

When you accept the change, your team will be right behind you. Address any gaps in skills and schedule training sessions to ensure the team is ready for the next step—brainstorming and developing an implementation strategy.

PLANNING

Develop a new strategy, a plan to ensure you are ready to implement the change. Lead by example; ensure you are modeling the proper behavior and your team is following you.

Life is ever-changing; every day we are faced with new initiatives and priorities, so without too much thought, start creating and setting goals.

Once everyone is on board, put on your best smile and task everyone independently to plan out how they will achieve the needed results with the new change. Then meet with the team to discuss and collaborate on the strategy to get everyone's buy-in. Encourage innovation and leverage feedback on new, creative ways to handle the change. This will get everyone on board and feeling supported. Then, collectively, you can move on to the next phase.

When COVID-19 struck and we had to change how we worked, as a leader I couldn't accept the change emotionally. I didn't feel safe—the unknowns, the uncertainty COVID-19 brought left me uneasy.

Many of our branches had to close. I went to speak to my manager, who reassured me we were taking all the measures necessary to ensure everyone was safe. I knew this, but I went to speak to him anyway because of my own fear. I talked to him two more times because I still needed reassurance and clarification. Under certain circumstances, you might have some emotional misgivings and find it hard to accept some changes. That's okay because you are human. But remember, talking about whatever is bothering you can help you get to a better place, and you will probably then feel there is a way out.

Remember, before you go onto implementation, ensure everyone is heard, everyone is on board, and you have everyone's buy-in for the new process.

> *"Teams that dream together of things yet to be, turn change into reality."*
> — Tracy Rohrer Irons

IMPLEMENTATION

Implementation is a very important step. Once you've ensured proper planning, it is your job to ensure the plan is implemented accurately and with zero errors. Without proper coaching and being intentional, the change will not be implemented correctly. You need to be present, not in your office working on other tasks, but on the floor with clear intentions.

You might have to do a lot of coaching here, for weeks or a couple of months, to ensure everyone is on board. Even if employees accept the change and collaborate in planning it, some might still have reservations deep inside that might show up during the execution.

In this situation, speaking only good words, you need to support and help the team members with training, hands-on experience, and observation. Continue to do one-on-one sessions or add more sessions for them until they are completely on board. Remember, people have their own learning styles and some may not be great at execution the first time. By being with them through all the steps, you and your team will implement the change successfully. Keep your head high.

RECOGNIZE THE CHANGE LEADERS

Volunteers: As soon as you are briefed on the change, print the necessary documents and schedule time to communicate the change with the team. Ask two or three team members if they would volunteer to participate in the presentation and give them small parts to play in the meeting. Prepare them to ensure they are comfortable. When the meeting ends, write personalized thank you cards to the team members who helped so they feel appreciated.

Trainees: When team members with a skills gap successfully complete training, recognize them with personalized thank-you cards and/or recognize them publicly, depending on their preference. (You will know this at the beginning of your relationship with them by asking how they want to be recognized.)

Team Members: Recognizing the team members who were knowledgeable about and on board with the change is very important. Make sure you thank them for their ongoing support with their choice of recognition.

PROGRESS RECOGNITION

It's important to recognize anyone who volunteers to help communicate the change at each meeting, on the spot, and or simply in your morning meetings. Ensure they know you have reached the specific learning milestone. Update everyone on the progress and thank them for their assistance in reaching that point.

IMPLEMENTATION DAY

Communicate with excitement. Bring in a fruit basket or flowers, depending on what's allowed in your workplace, and with great energy, start the implementation as a team. Celebrate the day, celebrate the changes, and send everyone an email, a card, and a verbal thank you for a job well done.

CELEBRATE THE SUCCESSFUL CHANGE

Once enough time has passed to work out any issues with the change and to see that it is working, it's time to celebrate the change. This last step of leading change is my favorite—celebrating with your team their hard work and the successful implementation.

EXERCISE

Once you've answered the following questions about change, go over them with your leader to see if there are any gaps or opportunities for more effectively implementing change.

1. Do you like change?
   _____
   _____

2. How do you communicate change to your team?
   _____
   _____

3. Do you own the change as a manager?
   _____
   _____

4. What do you do to get buy-in and raise excitement for the change?
   _____
   _____

5. Do you have a strong culture of celebrating achievements and effective change implementation?
   _____
   _____

6. How do you celebrate success?
   _____
   _____

This is your home, your culture of change you are creating. With a champion mindset, free of limitations, and by welcoming change with a smile, you will successfully overcome any challenges brought by the change. Remember to involve your team throughout the processes, watch for obstacles and negative reactions, and work on changing any negative perspectives to positive ones. Keep in mind, fear of the unknown is often the underlining issue with change; the unknown can be scary, or it can be beautiful. Scheduling events for the change project and holding employee training and meetings is key.

Now, let's dive into the next chapter where we talk about the most important person—the customer.

"Your most unhappy customers are the greatest source of learning."
— Bill Gates

CHAPTER 7

STEP 6 - BECOMING A CUSTOMER EXPERIENCE EXPERT

"While your company may offer a product or service, it is the experience you provide that truly defines your success."
— Jeff Bezos

Janet, the manager for a top food service supplier, was managing her team like a true legacy leader. She was a positive influence on her team and customers, leaving signs of excellence on anyone she interacted with. She always wore a smile, and her happy place was assisting her team in helping customers. She would greet everyone by name, and if she didn't know their name, she would say, "Welcome to our home. My name is Janet Jones; what is yours? Thank you for visiting us." Then she would have a relaxed, no pressure conversation with them. On Tuesdays, which were normally slow, she would call a random customer and invite them for coffee just to chat. It was called "Coffee with Janet." At first, her team thought it was a ridiculous idea; why would customers come in just for coffee? "Can we offer them a product or service?" they asked. "No," Janet replied. "I truly want us to get to know our customers and build a relationship and bond with them." No wonder she was number one in customer service in her region. Soon her team was as excited as she was about just having coffee with customers.

Here is a question to consider: How many people want to create relationships just to sell?

All the things we do in the background—the tasks and processes, the skills we learn, our own development, and developing our teams to strengthen them and make them experts in providing a seamless customer experience—are important when striving for customer loyalty. I believe it doesn't matter what product or service we provide or whether it's face-to-face with customers or working in the back office, one thing remains the same: You are dealing with a customer on the other end, and you must do it right every time to keep the customer happy; then they will be loyal for the long term. But is just doing it right enough? Let's review some important processes in your organizations.

Be present with your team to observe, coach, and develop them so they can get it right. I have seen many businesses where customers walk in and there is no management present or other backup for the team. I understand any company may have a lot of initiatives and projects going on, but can you work on them when your business is closed? If business owners, corporate personnel, and managers have limited time at work, hire an assistant manager or put other backup in place. You need to be present most of the time to know if your team is helping your customer properly and whether they go above and beyond. Without your help, they will be average or below average. You can ensure your team is above average simply by observing them, offering on-the-spot feedback, and providing regular coaching based on your observations. Continue this process until everyone on your team is consistently meeting your expectations and exceeding the customer's.

If your team provides phone- or internet-based services, it's essential to observe them to ensure they have excellent communication skills and to help them learn to go above and beyond.

FACE-TO-FACE CUSTOMER ENGAGEMENT

Ensure your team is fully engaging with customers and you have proper processes in place; then adjust processes until they are perfected. Follow your customer service protocol and transparently keep on top of all communications. Always follow company engagement practices because they are designed to ensure success, and your company has worked hard to design, test, and perfect them. To fully implement your customer engagement process or roadmap, work with the team member, coach them, and role-play until they understand it completely. Test their skills with face-to-face role plays. Instill in them the company initiative and ensure your team members connect with it. Creating a humanized, fun atmosphere is important to your customers and your team.

DON'T SAY NO, BUT PROVIDE OPTIONS

Adapt a high-energy persona with a happy, smiling voice, and lead with genuine concern for each challenge. We have various customers, and some can be more challenging than others. But what if a challenging customer asks for something beyond your reach? Would you say, "No, we don't do that"? To be an effective future leader, ensure your team provides options and seeks your guidance before saying no to customers. And always take and note customer feedback. Listening to our customers is essential. If we must say no to a customer, if we have listened and explored all the options we could possibly accommodate, striving to solve the problem, the customer will know we did our best to satisfy them. In the end, one of the options may be the one they wanted or needed to hear. Patience and willingness are the keys to solving customer problems, along with the character and emotion you put into working with that customer. When coaching your team, ensure you set them firmly on this road to success. And ensure the customer feels they have been heard and understood.

LEAD WITH VISION, GOING ABOVE AND BEYOND FOR CUSTOMERS

In the beginning of this chapter, I asked if doing right by the customer was enough. I believe we need to go beyond that, way beyond. You start by building rapport and then long-term relationships to gain and keep their loyalty. Only doing what is right for the customer and to their benefit is going above and beyond. Furthermore, it's essential to create a customer experience filled with respect, care, humility, and sincerity. You do that by creating a team culture based on emotional intelligence and empathy when interacting with customers.

Leading with a vision of creating the best customer experience requires developing yourself and your team's greatness. It also requires you to experience the customer experience before they do. You can start carving your vision by:

- Creating a customer experience culture with a highly emotionally intelligent team.
- Following by example and exhibiting all the necessary behaviors to make the customer your first priority.
- Demonstrating the ability to understand the customer's needs by asking the right questions.
- Providing coaching, development, and enthusiasm, and helping your team understand how to do it and why.
- Motivating, influencing, inspiring, supporting, and celebrating each accomplishment, from small to large.

Hug Your Customer and *Hug Your People* are two great books by Jack Mitchell, chair of Mitchell Stores. In them, Mitchell talks about your team needing to be treated well to be happy at work and how in response they will go above and beyond expectations. Mitchell's approach to customers was to treat everyone who came into the store like family.

Let's explore six behaviors your team needs to exhibit when helping customers and making them their top priority.

BEHAVIOR 1: DOING THINGS RIGHT AT ALL TIMES

By following the company's policies and procedures, your team can do things correctly at all times. Following the proper company policies and processes is a priority because they are the foundation of business practices. Doing things correctly and providing an exceptional customer service experience is the only formula for success. As an expert in this field, I have seen a lot of mistakes when teams are eager to help customers based on the pressures of meeting quotas or earning commissions. Ensure your team is always focused on leading and helping your customers to the customer's advantage. By creating a safe place with an environment that encourages always doing things right,

STEP 6 - BECOMING A CUSTOMER EXPERIENCE EXPERT

your compliant team is set for greatness. Sticking to your core values and being supportive is a win-win. Ensure you provide the needed support and encouragement.

BEHAVIOR 2: PUT THE RIGHT PEOPLE IN FRONT OF THE RIGHT CUSTOMERS

Developing and training teams to do the job effectively and be the expert is the only way to serve customers. It is unfair to team members and customers to put team members in the position of trying to serve customers without proper training and experience. Even if you are short-handed, find a team member with the proper expertise or help the customer yourself temporarily. Using underqualified team members will create more problems, and that's not fair to customers. I have seen this often. Just the other day when I was shopping, I asked a team member a question they couldn't answer—they were "just filling in." I never got the help I needed. Not a good look for the company.

In hiring for character, you want a diverse mix of people who complement and relate to one another. You also want people enthusiastic about your atmosphere and about supporting each other. Cross-train your team so they can work cross-functionally in all areas of your business, where applicable.

BEHAVIOR 3: GO ABOVE AND BEYOND IN HELPING CUSTOMERS TO EARN THEIR LOYALTY

Observe your team to ensure they exhibit proper behaviors and adhere to the customer-experience culture you've built. When a customer comes in, ensure team members:

- Walk toward the customer.
- Extend their hand to shake (unless prohibited or inappropriate for any reason).
- Make eye contact with the customer.
- Introduce themselves by name and area of expertise.
- Ask the customer how they can help them.

- Point the customer in the right direction and walk behind them.
- Pull a chair out for them.
- Make small talk and engage the customer.
- Find common interests and humanize them to create trust.
- Have a follow-through process.

Separate yourself from your competitors by what you do to make customers comfortable—know how are you raising the bar of customer experience.

From the least invested customer to the most, make everyone feel special and develop a lasting relationship; then in the long term, they will come back. This is how you develop longevity, great relationships, and continuing business for the company.

I met Nadia in 1996 at my first job. She was well-spoken, respectable, had great eye contact, a firm handshake, and was resilient. I thought, *There is nothing this employee can't do*. After twenty-seven years of a beautiful friendship, I called her to give me some insight on how she developed the customer experience she had been providing for decades. For years, Nadia had driven two hours to get to her job each morning and usually three hours home due to traffic. I asked her what motivated her to drive to Greenwich, Connecticut. She said it was how her manager treated her and her coworkers. Her manager made her feel like part of a family, which created a bond so strong she would drive five hours a day just to be there to help their customers and make her manager proud. I was astonished by her reaction to the treatment she received. I always say a loved one's house is never too far away, but for Nadia, a trip to her job was never too far.

BEHAVIOR 4: KNOW YOUR CUSTOMER

Knowing your customer is key to gaining their loyalty. Remember, customers come to see you and your team. Many businesses may offer similar services, but they want to see the caring Pat who goes above and beyond, the empathetic Avery who is an awesome listener, or the funny Blake who keeps them laughing and lightens their day.

Learn about their lifestyle, interests, and special days. Use this information to create special moments. Who are they and what do they do? What's important to them? Do they support a certain charity? If your company is planning a special event, you know whom to invite.

Loyalty builders include:

- Ensuring the customer experience is a top priority.
- Following through and reaching out on special occasions.
- Following up to ensure services are working well for them.
- Following up to connect in a way that makes them feel special.

BEHAVIOR 5: OVERCOME OBJECTIONS

Become familiar with common customer objections—price, product, and service—and create a culture of learning and collaboration for your team where they are safe to share their experiences and learn from each other. You can overcome objections by simply doing some basic exercises with your team that help create the trust needed so everyone can learn in a safe environment. Here are some exercises to try:

- Role-playing with your team helps ensure they can quickly overcome objections. With role-playing, repetition is key to learning.
- Brainstorming with groups, cross training, and introducing innovation will help teams bond and become more creative—helping them become the best version of themselves.
- Recording and recapping monthly meeting minutes and examining all the scenarios will help you develop best practices for the team.
- Celebrating each success when team members overcome objections raises morale and builds loyalty and job satisfaction.

BEHAVIOR 6: CREATE AN OBSERVANT CULTURE

The manager must observe team members to ensure they offer an excellent customer experience and exhibit the correct behaviors and skills. Observation is facilitated by the following tools and techniques.

- **Checklists:** Use a company observations checklist, or in a small business, create a checklist including the observations below—they are important to everyday interactions with customers. A well-rounded checklist will give you a clear picture of which team members exhibit exemplary customer service or which have some opportunities for improvement. You will be able to celebrate, encourage, and/or correct through your feedback. Give high-performing, satisfactory, and struggling team members feedback—we can sometimes forget to give continuous praise to people who get it right all the time. But it is important to recognize their efforts.

- **Greetings:** Observe team members as customers walk in to ensure they properly greet them. A proper greeting includes getting up and moving toward the customer, offering one's hand, as appropriate, and a properly friendly introduction and/or salutation. Once the team member leads the customer to the correct area, they should seat the customer while engaging in conversation geared toward learning about the customer and how to best help them. The customer experience should end with introducing the customer to the team and walking them to the door, displaying the utmost appreciation and gratitude. Ensure a proper follow-up process is in place and that the team member understands and follows it.

- **Customer Experience Roadmap:** Your job is to observe whether the team member follows the customer experience roadmap per company guidelines. If your company doesn't have something concrete, create your own customer experience roadmap outlining the ideal customer experience from start to finish, including all the questions team members need to ask. Include a section on common objections and how to overcome them. After observing team members, do one-on-one reviews and create a proper follow-up plan to bolster any weaknesses and reinforce positive traits.

- **Nonverbal Communication Skills:** Nonverbal communication is as important as verbal communication because it tells us if we are positive and eager to help our customers. Is our body language telling our customers we don't want to be bothered? Observe team members to ensure they display a warm, welcoming posture; they are observant and ready to help; and they have a happy smile, straight posture, and high energy.

- **Effective Communication Skills:** You must observe how your team communicates with customers. Watch for consistency with each customer. Depending on company policies and any limitation on sitting in on customer appointments, observing team members while they interact with customers can be the key to knowing if they communicate effectively. In the old days, my customers were happy when I sat in on their appointments. I made it part of our culture. I wanted to know my customers were receiving stellar service. I also had my leader sit in on my appointments to ensure I was meeting our high standards. The solid feedback I received helped me improve.

- **Active Listening:** Observe interactions to ensure your team listens to customers effectively, understands customer needs, and doesn't interrupt while the customer is talking.

- **Empathetic Response:** Observe your team to ensure they show empathy in conversation and exhibit empathetic responses. Role-play various scenarios and continue teaching teams because empathy is such an important soft skill when it comes to creating customer loyalty.

- **Overcoming Objections:** Continuously observe how your team overcomes objections. This is key to ensuring your team is well equipped with knowledge and resources. The best way to improve this skill is getting feedback and role-playing until team members have a full toolbox and can consistently handle any objection. Helen, one of my managers, held morning role-plays with her team before she opened the doors. She would invite me to give her feedback in case she missed anything. Together, we helped that branch get ranked at the top of our company's customer experience charts.

Remember, having great processes in place and cross-training your team to help where needed gives you the best chance to help your customers. By observing your team—focusing on the skills above—you can get the best customer experience and build a cohesive team, which will develop long-lasting relationships where everyone thrives.

> *"If you lose a client to someone else, it's because you didn't make the connection and deliver to that client's expectation. Keep in mind that the customer chooses you; it's an honor."*
> — Nadia Kappel

EXERCISE

1. Do you trust your team has customers' best interests in mind?
___
___

2. Do they know all the products and services you offer, and are they competent to execute them correctly?
___
___
___
___

3. Do you know all the products and services you offer customers in detail, and can you coach your team on these products/services efficiently?
___
___
___
___

4. List your thirty best customers. How many of their stories do you know?

5. In team meetings, have your team list their twenty best customers and write their stories. Which team member had less than twenty and why?

6. Do a brainstorming session with your team about overcoming objections, and write down the top ten they face. Then do a role-play of the ten. Invite your leader to be the customer. Come up with different scenarios. Make it fun and exciting, and mix your group. Lead by example, taking part in the exercise. How did your team do?

I hope you enjoyed the customer experience chapter and will incorporate the parts that stood out to you into your customer experience world. Now let's move on to Chapter 8, a very important chapter on an area I am very passionate about. It discusses the last job I did in corporate as a regional senior risk consultant, overseeing bank branches in different states with all their compliance components. I believe risk management should be the foundation for everything we do. It's doing things right when nobody's watching. Let's get excited, do some stretching, get some water, and then turn the page. Yay!

"Compliance is not about following regulations; it's about doing the right thing every single day."
— Sataya Naddella

CHAPTER 8

STEP 7 - DEVELOPING A RISK-MANAGEMENT CULTURE

"Risk comes from not knowing what you are doing."
— Warren Buffett

Victor ran his branch by ensuring customer experience was a top priority, and he hardly had any customer complaints. He felt he was following company policies and procedures, but he would not look at the actual company documentation of them to ensure he was doing the right thing. He just always felt he did, and he took a lot of pride in his customers always leaving happy. His numbers were always up, but his risk matrix indicators were suffering, and he didn't follow through by coaching his team when they made the same mistakes over and over again. Eventually, Victor was let go after much coaching and many warnings from his leader that the mistakes his team was making had to stop. What was Victor missing? Why wasn't Victor leading with risk management in the forefront of his mind?

As a regional senior risk consultant for a major bank, I was responsible for identifying, assessing, and effectively managing risk, compliance, and ensuring alignment with all aspects of the code of ethics and state regulations. I was astonished to find areas where the manager had failed to meet their responsibilities time after time. How can a manager turn a blind eye to such an important area? As hard as I tried to inspire some managers to see the vision and to help them develop new strategies, they still wouldn't make these areas a priority. My peers in different banks, companies, and locations had the same issues. My big question was: Why don't managers prioritize fixing something that is ruining their company's reputation, especially when integrity is so important today? Perhaps they just don't realize what they are doing, like Warren Buffet said—risk comes from not knowing what you are doing.

The foundation of any business is built on ensuring its operations align with the company's vision and a desire to do things correctly at all times.

To become a legacy leader, a person of utmost integrity, you need to ensure you and your team manage the risks in everything they do. Of course, we all want zero errors or omissions in our businesses, but that is impossible—we are human after all. Mistakes happen, but we shouldn't make the same mistake over and over again.

Here are four strategies to ensure everyone is on board with risk management:

STRATEGY 1: INSTILL A BELIEF IN MINIMIZING RISKS AND LEAD BY EXAMPLE

As a manager, you need to believe that risk management is part of your being. It's like the oxygen you breathe—you can't live without it. Here are three simple processes to monitor potential risks:

- Use a group calendar to schedule your inspections wherever they fit into the schedule to start the process and stay organized. A calendar is the best tool for ensuring you honor this responsibility and don't skip it.
- Take courses your company offers to fill in any skill gaps you may have.
- Find a peer in your market or region who is exemplary at risk management and reach out to them to see if they are willing to share best practices. Ask your leader or other top leaders in your business about mentoring you so you will have multiple resources when questions arise. When I first became a risk consultant, I had multiple peer mentors to help me learn best practices from multiple perspectives. In

STEP 7 - DEVELOPING A RISK-MANAGEMENT CULTURE

addition, I spent many days observing processes in action in different areas.

Through such processes, you can build relationships, gain multiple resources to tap into, and feel less alone while becoming the best leader possible when it comes to risk management.

Here are some best practices for becoming an unstoppable risk manager and dealing with any situation appropriately before it becomes unmanageable.

- **Monitor and analyze your business.** Ensure you keep a close eye to ensure processes are done correctly every day. Make it a best practice to observe the processes daily so you can manage them and correct them when needed through coaching and educating. That way you have an overall view of your day-to-day operation and how you conduct your business. I am aware that certain data is reported weekly or monthly, so in those instances, have the dates on your calendar to pull the reporting. Adopt a weekly or monthly analysis of your data and metrics, but have a daily view of how your team performed.

- **Identify the risk areas compromised.** If you identify any missed opportunities, take immediate action. Here you must be intentional. Do not put this task to the side, but face it head-on. Managers tend to identify the problem, but then they get sidetracked by internal or external factors and don't address the issue the same day. In such situations, ensure you schedule a one-on-one with the appropriate team member. In addition, if you have an assistant manager or a backup, include them in the meeting so they can cross-train and repeat what you would do in your absence so the two of you can become one unstoppable team.

- **Work on the area of opportunity immediately.** Once you have adopted the process and it is on your calendar for daily inspection, honor the time allotted to meet with your team member who needs extra help or clarification and your assistant or designated backup. Ensure you have a policy and procedure for the task to ensure your team member knows where to find the information. Looking up resources is a very important step as we will discuss later. Be sure to coach with a smile and you ask open-ended questions to find the root cause of the missed opportunity. Find out why the team member didn't follow the policy and whether they thought they did to ensure they will learn. Explain the procedure to them and provide them with resources for finding the correct information. Set up a follow-up meeting for a knowledge check to ensure the team member knows the right procedure. Third, invite the team member as a speaker to talk about the procedure in the upcoming monthly meeting. That way, they can teach other team members as an expert. By far, giving a team member the opportunity to learn and then teach others is the best way to keep a team member accountable. Then you are setting them up for future success.

- **Create a spot check program.** Make sure you follow up on missed risk metrics from time to time to be certain the team has learned and adopted the task. Between you and your assistant or backup, create an ongoing calendar to follow up to determine the area needing improvement is no longer a concern. By implementing a spot check, you create a culture of awareness and standards that will prepare you, your team, and your company for ongoing success.

> *"The essence of risk management lies in maximizing the areas where we have some control over the outcome while minimizing the areas where we have absolutely no control over the outcome."*
> — Peter L. Bernstein

STRATEGY 2: SET YOUR FOUNDATION WITH YOUR EMPLOYEES AND INSTILL UNIFORM BELIEFS

New team member training programs should allow sufficient time to learn every aspect of their job and their priorities as risk managers. Once they have learned all risk indicators, they need to shadow another team member until they are 100 percent ready to start. New employees can ruin the company's

STEP 7 - DEVELOPING A RISK-MANAGEMENT CULTURE

reputation if they start before they are ready—so don't put them in the game before they are fully trained, even if you have limited staff. Firing an ill-trained team member because their manager had them start too soon is unfair and allows the manager to repeat this mistake in the future. I have seen cases like this throughout my career. Handle new team members with the care and respect they deserve, and give them time to learn before they are put on the floor to represent your company. In guarding their success, you guard your brand and reputation.

Following are three ways to guard your employees' success, and your brand and reputation by extension:

- **Manage risks so they don't happen.** Zero risk would be amazing, but it's impossible. However, if you work *toward* the goal of zero, you will end up with minimal risks, and that is exemplary. Teach your team best practices from the beginning, train them, and develop them so they know how to manage risk within their roles and responsibilities. Ensure you go over the specifics of their job and they understand their responsibilities. Explain the consequences of noncompliance with and/or poor execution of company guidelines so there are no surprises. Risk management, complete and accurate compliance, and a firm code of ethics are not to be taken lightly. With daily communication and transparency on these topics, consistency in updating the team on new initiatives, and implementing the changes correctly in a timely manner as one team, you and your team can do wonders in controlling risk.

- **If an error occurs, ensure you have a coaching culture in place.** As I said earlier, risk excellence is your foundation, your house, and if policies are broken, or your team is not paying attention to them, you need to ensure you have a coaching culture in place to correct the problem. This coaching should be ongoing and timely. Schedule a one-on-one session, and bring the team member into a safe coaching environment. Speak with a caring voice, great posture, empathy, and compassion. Find the root of the problem, and ask open-ended questions to ensure they know what the problem was, why it's important, and exactly what error they made. No matter how big or small the mistake was, ensure you listen to your team member without interrupting. Make sure they feel heard. Create a collaborative action plan to work out solutions and steps for going forward. Before the meeting ends, schedule a follow-up that fits your team member's schedule. With consistent coaching and a coaching culture in line with your company's core values, you can help team members grow. And you set yourself up as a strong leader doing their job well.

- **When a team member continues to ignore policies and procedures, you must take decisive action.** Sometimes team members continue to break the rules by not paying attention to policies and/or making the same mistakes over and over again. Managers keep coaching them on the same actionable item without positive results. If this happens, you should have documented coaching conversations and be ready to take action, including termination. If you have to terminate, don't let your emotions get the best of you; remain calm and maintain your normal mannerisms. I have seen managers become frustrated at this stage and fail to conduct themselves respectfully. You can't show your frustration. Remember, you're the leader. You need to show empathy and compassion in all situations. As long as you have diligently put in the work along the way and taken every opportunity to turn the team member around, it's not your fault. The job might not have been the right fit. Let them go with respect and dignity. In the end, they know they failed.

> *"Sense and deal with problems in their smallest state,
> before they grow bigger and become fatal."*
> — Pearl Zhu

STRATEGY 3: REDUCE RISK BY BEING AUDIT READY EVERY DAY

Developing a strong team that is audit ready every day is the best way to be compliant and know you and your team are exhibiting all the necessary behaviors for creating a safe and risk-free environment. As I said, everyone is a risk manager, and everyone must follow company policies and procedures. If you were audited today by internal or external auditors, would you pass easily? If your area was audited while you were on vacation, would you worry or feel confident your team was ready and would pass with a high score? These are two important questions to consider when managing risk, so be brave, work hard, and be ready for whatever life brings because, at the end of the day, you are your team's quality control officer.

Two important ways to ensure you are always audit ready are:

- **Create risk champions.** You don't have to do it all alone. You can and should delegate and cross-train your team. Designate champions for the different risk areas. Hold a risk management brainstorming meeting and ask for volunteers to be champions in the various areas. In addition, be innovative, share ideas, and ask, "What programs can we develop and implement within your champion area to get our desired outcomes?" Know that you have created a great team of innovators who love the diversity and inclusiveness you foster. They are cohesive, smart, cross-trained, and care deeply about your company's success. Choosing champions from this pool of talent should lead to successful risk management plans.

- **Have champions monitor their areas.** Monitoring will give your champions the leadership experience they need to set them on a path to greatness. In identifying champions, you will see who is so passionate, who needs more work, and who wants to be developed to move into their next role. It is your duty to ensure you see their talents and elevate them to a greater purpose.

STRATEGY 4: CELEBRATE YOUR TEAM'S SUCCESSES

From small achievements like knowing where to find a particular policy to big ones like passing an audit with a high score, as a manager, it's up to you to celebrate your team's accomplishments when it comes to risk management. Show your team how proud you are of them.

Some ways to celebrate your employees include:

- On the spot when they follow a policy or procedure.
- By sending e-cards with positive messages about their risk management successes.
- Sending a handwritten note.
- Recognizing a team member in a meeting.

EXERCISE

1. Identify the three top risks in your office and create a detailed strategy to mitigate each. Record the risks here and call the mitigation plan a special project. Make it a thirty-day project. Pick team members who would be great champions for each risk. Provide resources and create a safe place for the team and champions to learn. Follow up on the project's progress weekly. This exercise will empower your team, strengthen their skills, and give them a path to greatness. Coaching is a great way to develop future leaders, but taking a champion (leadership) role in these kinds of projects is a different and effective way to learn and grow. Try it.

_____

_____

_____

Next, let's dive into how to show our company we are working toward our goals, we are successful producers, and we are profit-driven leaders. Let's go!

"If you want to have a profitable business, you need to have an efficient business."
— Hendrith Smith

CHAPTER 9

STEP 8 - BECOMING A PROFIT-DRIVEN LEADER

*"The business has only two functions—
marketing and innovation. All the rest are costs."*
— Peter Drucker

Miranda is a high-performing manager and profit-driven leader. She grew her brand by increasing revenue and reducing costs. She built a strong, diverse, and cohesive culture by developing and influencing her team to succeed every day. Her day starts by analyzing data and looking at patterns, trends, and opportunities. She has strong financial acumen, enabling her to make strong, informed decisions and strategize projects according to the data. She is adept at assessing risks and understands the importance of following company and regulatory guidelines. She is great at allocating resources to where they are needed most. Miranda stays on top of daily communication, is a great listener in her meetings, and always takes notes. She adopts best practices from her peers no matter where they are. She simply calls to get their insight. She is also a great mentor and does not rest on her success. Instead, she continuously looks for innovations to strengthen her cohesive team. She has developed and maintains a positive vision, and she knows her team can get there.

We would all love to have a leader like Miranda in our company. She has all the success-generating traits a leader should have. To lead like Miranda and drive company revenue, you need to think like a leader and have a vision to fulfill based on ensuring the company's success. Thinking like a leader means consistently working to ensure you, your employees, and the company succeed to the extent your role can influence success. Always think like a leader and you will be successful.

To transform managers into leaders and maximize profits, you need a great mindset and to follow the following processes. They are the non-negotiables that drive revenue.

HAVE POSITIVE MINDSET AND A WELL-DEFINED VISION

Have a positive mindset in every aspect of your business. You signed up to do a great job, and you are obligated to do so. You have the skills and ability to get there as we discussed. I find failing to live up to your obligations unacceptable. If you commit to something, you need to step up and fulfill that promise. Some fail due to poor planning and/or organization. I understand many companies have challenging goals, but they usually also have a company direction, resources, and a roadmap to get there. With a positive mindset, believing you and your team are up to the challenge, you can achieve your goals.

Know your business. Know your business and be excited to analyze reports daily. When you are excited, curious, and full of positive energy, you will make a difference and drive results. Share your excitement with your team. To know your business, follow your patterns and trends, and when you see an opportunity, work on taking advantage of it with your team. Involve your team in planning and thinking up innovative solutions—unleash your team's creativity.

Once you have a clear picture of where you are and where you want to go, with your collaborative team behind you, work on the change until you get the desired results. Striving to bring in revenue in each area requires you to be intentional and know what you need to work on. Once you know your business, you are halfway there. You will be quick to analyze and change directions with consistency and discipline.

Embrace failures as a necessary part of learning. Your vision might fail a few times. That's okay. Keep your positive mindset. Think of it as being closer to succeeding on your next try. Try different ways, make new plans, and leverage your resources. Your team is your biggest strength and the resource to start with. By empowering your team, holding ongoing brainstorming sessions with them, and creating group activities and exercises, your team will think more and more like you. Other resources you can tap into include peers, upper management, and outside sources like business organizations. Of course, you have to keep your skills up to date to remain relevant, so lean into continuing education throughout your career.

Create a high-performance team. A high-performance team is crucial to growing your business, bringing in revenue, and replicating positive results over and over again. You want to ensure every team member is trained and producing optimally. Remember, you are building this team and developing each member to be the best version of themselves in every respect. That means they consistently execute their tasks and perform to the highest standards of excellence. Everyone is on board and positive, working toward the desired outcome. Depending on the circumstances, if you see someone falling short, you need to recognize it and get them back on track by exhibiting empathy, providing all the necessary coaching and follow up, and providing them with resources. In addition, creating mentorship programs to team them up with other high-performing team members is great for continuous education. To achieve substantial growth and success for the company, you need to create a cohesive, thriving environment that screams success, with each team member doing their utmost to be successful. Everyone has achieved great success and owes a piece of that growth to working together with you and the team.

Set strategic goals. Setting goals is not about aiming for the requirements but pushing way beyond that. You want your team to think about exceeding expectations by innovating and creating. Include everyone in planning, and tap into their insights to ignite their greatness. Set goals together with your team. Never settle for the minimum. Strive to be the best and most successful team. Who can create that kind of champion mindset in a team? As the leader, along the way always plant the seed that they can achieve anything they put their minds to. Create a safe place where everyone cares about each other's success because that success is the company's success.

Embrace new technology. Efficiency helps grow revenue. Keep up with the times and introduce every new technology that can speed up your processes or reduce errors. Customers want to be in and out and not have to wait too long, so to reduce wait time, ensure you have the most advanced technology to serve them efficiently. The same goes for all internal processes—invest in updated technology for a quicker turnaround. Ensure everyone is on board—in with the new and out with the old. Provide the training and resources needed and help the team adapt to the new technology. If someone is set in their ways, work with them to help them get there.

Leverage your partners. Partners in this context are people in your organization or field with expertise in various areas related to your work. They see you as a valuable resource, so the relationship is mutually beneficial—a partnership. You exchange knowledge. We all have partners who are experts in a given field. Ryan was one of my managers who was known for partnering with others, tapping into their expertise to gain insights and find better ways to do things. Ryan always had a partner to help enhance his business acumen and improve his team. If you shy away from asking for help, stop it. Start asking, no matter how successful you are. You can have partners from any area of the business who can help you become even more successful. Partnering is a great skill. It helps you build strong bonds and relationships and continuously improve your skills and knowledge. Invite partners to meetings, invite them to your shared celebrations, and make them part of your team. My manager Ryan invited partners to recurring meetings each month. In most cases, everyone wants to share their knowledge and offer their services. It's a win-win—you learn and improve your skills/knowledge, and they get to share their expertise.

Nurture customer relationships. Without our customers, we don't have businesses. They are the final stage of our operation. No matter how great your processes are, if your roadmap doesn't lead to a successful sale, you don't

STEP 8 - BECOMING A PROFIT-DRIVEN LEADER

have an effective process. In addition, repeat business comes from nurturing existing customers, which usually leads to gaining new ones—word of mouth is great marketing. If you don't have one, create your customer service roadmap, ensuring your processes go above and beyond customer expectations. Once developed, ensure everyone is on board with executing it. Following a well-thought-out roadmap is a big part of profit-driven success.

Amber and Sherry were managers and top performers in their region. They loved healthy competition and wanted to provide an exemplary customer experience. They followed their sales numbers daily, striving to stay on top in their region. They called each other every day, excited to see who was on top. They regularly celebrated with their teams and brought them together at the company's annual celebration. They took this opportunity to learn best practices from each other. They stayed organized by meticulously using their calendars.

Stay organized. Being organized is vital to success. Here is how you can stay organized like Amber and Sherry.

- **Daily:** Monitor your data, analyze it, and make sure you know it well to identify areas of opportunity. Brainstorm your plan for the day.

- **Weekly:** Hold formal brainstorming sessions and use your resources to innovate. Empower your team to be innovative in offering new strategies.

- **Monthly:** Conduct meetings to discuss all aspects of your area of the business. Analyze the data and prepare reports so your team understands the current situation and trends. Assign a team member to each area of concern and/or opportunity. Invite partners to support you in the meeting. Ensure your agenda has a little part included for everyone to contribute. Get help from your leader if you are organizing an initial meeting.

- **Quarterly:** Ensure you are where you need to be for the quarter. Look at gaps and define a strategy with your team to correct any insufficiencies.

- **Bi-Yearly:** Identify how you are doing at mid-year and what you need to adjust to get where you need to be. Look up your patterns, gaps, and opportunities to improve. Hold a meeting to discuss progress and the areas that need improvement. Develop strategies and goals to meet your objectives.

- **Annual goal:** Pull your annual data and use it to reflect on what transpired in each area of your business. Meet with your team to update everyone on how well you've met your performance matrix. I am sure you worked strategically toward your goal and reflected on the processes that got you there.

- **Use a shared calendar:** It's a great way to schedule your weekly, monthly, quarterly, by-yearly, and annual meetings to review your performance and drive business results. Staying organized, scheduling each event appropriately, and honoring your calendar will help you be intentional about making decisions and driving revenue appropriately. You are carving your path to success and walking with clear intent. This means you know where you are with sales, recognize gaps and opportunities, and have an improvement strategy. Planning your entire year helps you know exactly what you need to do to meet annual goals and measure incremental results. Be diligent and intentional about meetings, empowering everyone to have a voice and giving them a positive atmosphere and a safe place to think.

- **Hit your goals:** Hold yourself and your team accountable to higher standards. We all have choices about where we work. Once we have chosen, we have an obligation to the health of our company to hold ourselves and our team accountable for our performance. We need to grow our business and create a path for getting there with our teams.

Your team will be as successful as you are when you work together with them, creating high standards and not deviating from them. By following all the processes, holding yourself and your team accountable, coaching them along the way, and adjusting where needed, you will meet your quotas month after month, year after year. I wish you the greatest success.

STEP 8 - BECOMING A PROFIT-DRIVEN LEADER

CELEBRATE ACHIEVEMENTS

It's time to celebrate your achievements. You worked strategically with your team and had a clear path. Hold great goal-hitting celebrations quarterly, bi-yearly, and annually. First, brainstorm ideas with your team and collectively choose to go out to a favorite or new restaurant (inviting their plus ones) or have a potluck party where everyone brings in their favorite dish for others to try. In addition, write a big certificate of honor for everyone because everyone was part of your success and deserves a piece of the celebration.

EXERCISE

1. Write your new, innovative process for how you and your team will drive profits and hit all your monthly, quarterly, and yearly goals. Reflect on how you can get your entire team to be top performers and drive revenue for your business.

_____
_____
_____
_____

Now let's look at the ninth step toward becoming a legacy leader by becoming responsible for our own development. We are almost there. Let's go!

"Leaders inspire accountability through their ability to accept responsibility before they place blame."
— Courtney Lynch

CHAPTER 10

STEP 9 - BECOMING RESPONSIBLE FOR YOUR OWN DEVELOPMENT

"When you think everything is someone's fault, you will suffer a lot. When you realize that everything springs only from yourself, you will learn both peace and joy."
— Dalai Lama

Who is the most important person in helping you get to your next desired position?

Let me tell you a story about a hardworking manager named Aisha who consistently went beyond her duties with a smile on her face.

Aisha was a manager under my supervision. I coached her. We had weekly check-ins and monthly meetings to go over her progress. We created a plan for her to become the leader she always wanted to be. I had her shadow me and join in my district visits, and I engaged her in doing audits and inspections with me. She was doing excellently. An opportunity came up—an opening for an operational consultant. I was excited and told her, "Aisha, get ready; here is your chance."

Aisha replied, "I am so confused. I don't know where to go. One day I want to work in HR, and the next day I want to work in operations. But I feel like I'll fail wherever I go because I don't have time. My family needs me."

That happens to all of us when we have many passions. Aisha told me in confidence that since coming to the United States from Egypt, she hadn't had a role model to assess her skills. I know Aisha lacked confidence in her abilities because she was pulled in so many directions. And she was a people pleaser who often focused on others' needs—to the point where she was passing up a great opportunity to get her dream job.

Aisha needed to work on herself.

You must believe in yourself unconditionally, even in hard times. You can become the great leader you always wanted to be, no matter where you come from or how heavy your accent is. You are born with natural abilities and talents you can build on and use to help your team. Have you asked yourself the hard questions? What is preventing you from being promoted at work? Is it because you didn't have opportunities? Have you interviewed but been told they went with another, more qualified candidate?

I have been there, and the doubts and rejection led me to doing a thorough self-evaluation. I took a hard look at my mental state and skills. I realized one thing: The only person responsible for my development was *me*. It is easy and natural to look for causes outside ourselves. We don't want to believe we just weren't good enough or didn't try hard enough. So, we stay in the background, feeling hurt, angry, and resentful. Often, we are afraid to take a chance, so we self-sabotage just as Aisha did with her limiting beliefs. She was so talented and intelligent that the only reason she couldn't do anything she wanted to do was thinking she couldn't do it.

Have you truly asked yourself what is preventing you from getting your dream job? Ask yourself, "What steps have I taken to get close to my goal?" For example, have you asked other professionals who care about you, your coworkers, or your leaders for help? Have you asked them which skills they think you might need to strengthen? Have you asked others what they think about you as the next leader? Ask family, close friends, or peers who are doing well, or other senior leaders you have worked with on a project for their feedback.

This is how I did it: I asked for feedback in every interaction or meeting I spoke at, even from people I did not know. Before I was promoted to my consultant job, I had to push myself out of my comfort zone. I used to be so nervous, but I had to push through that edge to become who I am today.

A while back, I read an article by Michael Falcon on LinkedIn that truly resonated with me and fits this chapter well. Falcon said:

> I will never stop learning because I'm scared I will become obsolete or irrelevant. I recently spoke with someone who I can only assume was in their 50s or 60s. "I'm too old to be studying," he proclaimed. This person is dying, maybe not physically, but professionally, they are dead. Educating yourself doesn't end after university or when you're in the early years of your career. Regardless of age, you must continue growing and developing yourself.

It's so true. We can never stop learning no matter what age we are.

Let me take you through twelve actions that helped me become responsible for my own development.

ACTION 1: OVERCOME SELF-IMPOSED BARRIERS

Eliminate success blocks like thinking you are not good enough; self-sabotaging; focusing on being a minority, too old, or too young; thinking you can't compete against "more qualified" people, etc.

You can crush your limiting beliefs through personal development, getting a life coach, and/or listening to any of the many great motivational speakers.

ACTION 2: CREATE A VISION BOARD

Create a vision board of where you want to be. My vision was to become a legacy leader filled with empathy and compassion. No matter how many leadership styles I had, this one was embedded in my DNA. It is how I was raised, how I loved people at home, and how I identify my blocks. I wanted to bring this feeling into my work and help others do the same. My vision was to become a leader—I imagined it, I modeled it, and I invested time into it. I truly enjoyed my life managing and developing others, but I wanted to help more people by transforming managers into leaders focused on risk management who know how to develop diverse talent. After my last manager role, I transformed into the leader of my dreams. I knew it was time because I had no doubts. I knew I was ready because I was mentally prepared and I had worked on every skill I was told needed strengthening. At last, I got my dream job.

ACTION 3: ADD A TIMEFRAME

Define how long it will take to reach your goal. Time is an important component because it allows you to plan your route to success and set milestones along the way so you can check in on your progress. That gives you the chance to celebrate incremental achievements, which adds discipline—you have to track and meet deadlines.

If you are a seasoned manager, you should only need three to six months to get to your next desired position. If you feel you need more time to get your mind, body, and soul in gear, give yourself six to nine months. Your timeline depends on your personality. Assess what you need to learn and give yourself a fair shot. But let's schedule your date!

ACTION 4: USE A CALENDAR

Put your timeframe on your calendar. I've often heard, "If you do not put it in your calendar, it will not happen."

How do you schedule time for yourself and your development when you are very busy with daily tasks and deadlines? Do it by scheduling time for development on your calendar—weekly and monthly—and respecting that time. Schedule time for yourself. Enter all the activities you need to do, including daily meditation, affirmations, visualization, exercise, and work responsibilities. Schedule your time from waking until bedtime. At first, you may think it's too much, but it's a necessary practice and helps prepare you to use a calendar every day for the rest of your life. I use my iPhone. It's easy for me. Select whichever method works for you.

ACTION 5: ENGAGE YOUR LEADER

Have you had a one-on-one with your manager to help you with your vision? Have you told them what your fear is and your limitations? Coming to a different country is scary no matter how many years you are here. For me, it is thirty years, and it took me almost two decades to conquer my fears. Tell your leader in three to six months, or two years, or whatever makes sense in your situation that you want to become a leader. Ask which skills you need to have and work on them. You might be good at some, with others needing some work. One skill I needed to work on was listening.

ACTION 6: KNOW YOUR SKILLS

Knowing your skills and competencies is half the battle. As I mentioned above, get your leader's feedback and take a hard look at yourself—you know yourself and which skills you need. Then start working on them. Going back to my listening skills, I needed help from an expert, not a coworker, and my leader set me up with his peer from another area. My issues were that I interrupted people, and I got bored in long meetings and started multitasking, which I thought made me a super-worker. It did not. Less than a year after receiving coaching from the best, I learned to listen actively and focus on the person or people in front of me. With practice and awareness, I continue to improve each day. I give people time, and I listen without interrupting.

ACTION 7: PARTNER WITH A MENTOR

Find and partner with someone who is great at the skill you need to strengthen. It can be a peer from another area, a senior leader, or someone else you see as a mentor. Ensure you spend enough time with them to learn the skill before moving on to the next. I met with my mentor once a month, and I had exercises to do in between.

ACTION 8: SPEND TIME WITH PEOPLE YOU CAN LEARN FROM

Whom do you want to spend your time with? What do you do on weekends, and whom do you do it with? Maybe it is time to reassess how you spend your time. If you want to be a leader, surround yourself with people who can teach you something, who can better you in some way. This will help you develop and reach for more. Find groups that elevate your mind, your spirit, and your growth. Often spending a lot of time in the same circle can stunt your growth and impede learning. Reassess to see if each group you spend time with is still serving you well. Then search for a great learning companion. Reach out to educational groups and volunteer for causes you believed in. Surround yourself with trusted friends and people you can learn from who care about your development.

By following these principles and strategies and becoming responsible for your own development, you are ready to start searching for the leadership job you always wanted. Let's now look at some areas you need to focus on to be ready for an interview.

ACTION 9: KEEP YOUR RESUME UPDATED AT ALL TIMES

When creating and updating your resume, ask your leader to help you, take a resume writing course, get help from a friend, or go to a reputable company for help updating it. Also, keep your resume in front of your scenario book and update your accomplishments as you achieve them so you stay current.

ACTION 10: WRITE YOUR BIO

It is helpful to write your biography because "Tell us about yourself" is a common interview question. When you speak with someone at a work function or networking event, you can highlight the benefits of your skills. You never know whom you will be speaking with or whom you can impress. I landed a job that way at the beginning of my career—I was recruited due to an interaction with someone from a different company.

ACTION 11: NAIL THE INTERVIEW

How can you nail the interview and get the job? You may say, "It's not as easy as it sounds." You are not alone since many people fear interviews. That fear is common at every level of management, especially for those who stay in a role for a long time and have not interviewed in many years.

Now, many businesses and corporations use the SAR (situation, action, and result) interview format. I am sure you are familiar with it; it is a behavioral interview where you need to describe a situation, what action you took, and the result. It is based on real-life scenarios that you need to come up with. Depending on the company, it can be anywhere from five to ten scenarios.

Some things that helped me through this process for you to consider are:

1. Be observant while you work, especially when you come across a good scenario, and jot it down so you do not forget it.
2. Set up a scenario book where you record different scenarios.
3. Stay organized and update your scenario book often. For example, when you solved problems, when you went above and beyond for a customer, when you developed a team member, or when you learned a new skill.
4. Keep practicing. This will mitigate your fear of interviews and enable you to apply for a job when it is available.

The key is to make this task a priority for your development and schedule it into your everyday life.

ACTION 12: CELEBRATE MILESTONES WITH YOUR LOVED ONES

Celebrating yourself is as important as celebrating others. Let your love and the efforts you made shine forth. Remember to give yourself grace and have your loved ones celebrate with you. I celebrate any achievements, mine and theirs, with my friends and family. As important as working hard is, it's just as important to have fun, excitement, and joy in your life. Live it up!

> *"You must believe in yourself and start carving*
> *your own path to your greatness!"*
> — Zana Kenjar

Let's sum up this chapter with some affirmations and then do an exercise to help you with self-development.

Recite these daily affirmations for twenty-one days to help you get there:

- I believe in myself strongly and unconditionally, even in hard times.
- I will create a vision board of where I want to go.
- I will get my leader position by (fill in the blank).
- I will use a daily calendar to schedule all my events.
- I will engage my leader and hold them and myself accountable for my development.
- I will assess my skills and work on any I, my leader, and my mentor think need strengthening.
- I will partner with an amazing mentor and great communicator.
- I will spend time with people I can learn and grow with.

Experts say after twenty-one days any activity becomes a habit.

EXERCISE

1. Write a letter to the future you—the future diversified leader who has so much love and empathy for others, leads with the mission of developing people, and listens to others' perspectives. Think big for yourself—remember, you crushed your limitations and now you are free to reach for the sky. Your possibilities are endless. Let the Universe work for you. All you have to do is declare your intension with a strong will and conviction. Then read this letter as often as you can. Be creative and have fun with it. Stay within your vision!

   Start with:

   Dear Me,

   You have succeeded! You are enjoying your role as a leader and helping many managers....

_____
_____
_____
_____
_____

I hope you love your future letter and read it every day, while visualizing the great life ahead of you.

Now let's look at the tenth and final step in becoming a legacy leader—where you will win your interview, get your leadership job, and get ready to create future leaders. I am so excited for you. Let's go!

"The mark of a great leader is not just their ability to lead, but their ability to develop and empower others to lead."
— Jack Welch

CHAPTER 11

STEP 10 - LEADERS CREATE FUTURE LEADERS

"A leader is like a shepherd. He stays behind the flock, letting the most nimble go out ahead, whereupon the others follow, not realizing that all along they are being directed from behind."
— Nelson Mandela

Let's look at the scenario below to see if you resonate with this successful manager who is ready for the next leadership role.

You were away for a week of training for your next leadership role. When you return to your office, you see all of your favorite employees and notice their diverse backgrounds. All the people you hired have one thing in common: great character! They are all amazing—they help each other, no one is left behind, and they have fun all day working and ensuring they help their customers reach their goals. They make you proud. You walk in already knowing you are above your goals in every category, and you know they all go above and beyond to help the customer and build loyalty. Your employees are so happy to see you, and they can't wait to hear about your training and tell you about the audit they passed with ease. You are overwhelmed with joy just seeing them, and you feel very proud of the cohesive and collaborative team you developed. You feel you have done all you could for everyone, and you have been very successful for years in developing yourself and your team and growing your company's revenue year after year.

Would you like to have a high-performing team that is collaborative, cares about the customers, and collectively helps each other?

Behind this team is a strong, caring leader who leads with empathy and compassion and wants to leave a mark of greatness on everyone. This leader is responsible for their own development and is ready to take their next step into leadership.

I recently read the article "Five Things to Look for in Future Leaders" by Jay Richards. This article resonated with me so much. Richards' says the main reason people leave their company is their boss. It's true. My friend's husband just left his job for that reason. He loved the company but his boss wasn't a leader. The article says effective leaders should possess five attributes:

1. Earns the confidence and trust of others
2. Engages others in ways that ensure buy-in and commitment
3. Builds effective teams and gets the job done
4. Serves as a model for creating change in other parts of the organization
5. Provides employees with a clear mission.

We have talked about all of these and their importance in developing leadership skills. Now let's see how you can adopt these qualities.

ADOPT THE QUALITIES AND BEHAVIOR OF A LEGACY LEADER

Let's look at a much more surprising story. Recently, I was invited to a graduation party at my friend's house. I was excited to go because we had mutual friends, and I thought I would see some familiar faces. I recognized a few people. Then I saw Linda, an old employee from decades earlier, talking to a woman I didn't recognize. As I was about to approach, I heard Linda saying, "This woman was my first manager at a department store. If it wasn't for her, I wouldn't have the lifestyle I have, the house I bought, and traveled as I did. I owe this woman and so many others."

Linda was talking about me! I was so surprised I had made such a difference in people's lives, and after two decades, Linda still remembered. I thought I had just done the right thing at the time. I led with my heart and was willing to help anyone who was breathing, both in my personal and professional life. I had been carrying a legacy leader within and didn't even know it.

Before I heard Linda and many others say the same thing, I didn't realize I was a legacy leader. I had left marks on others one by one without intending to, just from a pure love for developing and directing others' successful lives.

At the time, I was still writing this book and battling with my title. I had thought it might be *The Power of Empathetic Leadership* because I wanted to instill empathy to create more love in the world. But regardless of whether empathy is a critical skill or a soft skill, we need so much more than that. We need empathy to take an interest in and put ourselves in others' shoes, but we also need to help people with their problems through compassion. I wanted these leaders I was helping to build to have it all—to shine, become unstoppable, love unconditionally, go above and beyond, and stretch! I wanted to transform the leader who has all the qualities but needs a little push, a direction. I have seen so many managers struggle to build cohesive teams, or to have great teams but find something blocks their success in moving on to the next role—fear holds them back.

In recapping the processes we've talked about throughout this book, I want you to know my intent is for you to have a meaningful life with all the joy you deserve. Know that there are ten important steps to becoming a legacy leader who will make a major difference in other people's lives and your own. Your team will be so grateful when you show them a path to greatness, and you will receive all the blessings for getting them there. Your mark will be more fulfilling than money alone can reflect. Positive intentions bring positive results and a happy life. The key is to live in humility and always practice sincerity.

Let's review what we have learned. This chapter is about how leaders create other leaders, but first you have to become a leader yourself, so here are the Ten Steps to Becoming a Legacy Leader:

STEP 1: BUILD YOUR CHAMPION MINDSET

Believe you can achieve whatever you set your mind to. To cultivate that belief you need to:

- **Remove any success blocks, including fear:** Release any beliefs like, "I am not good enough for that job. I still have a long way to go, and my manager doesn't care about my development." Release that and don't let old junk live in your soul. Such thoughts are often untrue—we make them up. Even in your personal life, let go of old hurts. It's old, and the person who hurt you didn't know any better at the time. Remove such thoughts by getting into a healthy routine—wake up early, exercise, pray, meditate, and recite affirmations for whatever pain you can't let go of. If you feel you give too much or you are not enough, listen to affirmations of self-love or abundance and repeat. That will reprogram your mind to believe those positive words, and they will become true. Be consistent. Visualize the great life ahead of you; feel it as if it's already here. In a leadership position, if you are sitting in your office or talking to your team, keep visualizing great success and it will happen—consistency and repetition is key.

- **Develop Self-Awareness:** Be aware of yourself, including your strengths and weaknesses, and ask questions. Invite more feedback from others to find things you are not aware of. Plan questions and have the discipline to execute. The best way to get to your leadership role is to be honest about what you need to focus on developing to get to the desired destination.

STEP 2: BUILD YOUR WINNING TEAM

Hire people with character, and teach them the needed skills; they will work hard when you work hard back. Align your team's efforts with overall organizational objectives. Build trust and respect with everyone, and create unity and a collaborative safe atmosphere where everyone can learn and grow. Inspire you team to greatness, and treat everyone as you would your family. This is the easiest formula to remember. Celebrate everyone as you would celebrate your family from the smallest to biggest accomplishment. Show empathy and compassion for your team as you would show your family, and ensure you create options for everyone to be successful. We love our families and we stretch for them. Do the same and stretch for your team; they will know and appreciate you. Practice these processes and you will have a cohesive team. With collaboration and a positive and loving atmosphere, your company's success and revenues will multiply.

STEP 3: FOSTER DIVERSITY AND INCLUSION

Learn more about building diversity and inclusiveness. Ensure everyone has a sense of belonging to one happy team, knows they are heard, and that you are providing an inclusive and safe environment to learn in. Develop relationships with your team and understand their worldviews. Always maintain a culture in which everyone respects everyone and embraces who they are.

Inspire your team and motivate them. Be innovative, and give them the autonomy to think out loud, find their uniqueness, and understand what makes them shine.

STEP 4: LEAD WITH INFLUENCE

Master the art of influence and you will be very successful. The words you utter should only be loving words—words that would positively land on someone without fear. Words can inspire us to do great things, so ensure your communication is at its best. Leading by example, ensure your words match your actions. Always pay attention to your body language, your nonverbal influence. Don't let your title get the best of you. Don't be afraid to get your hands dirty. No task is beneath you. You are part of your team and should have the willingness to go the extra mile. Show your team members the way to get to their desired destinations, and see the best in them.

STEP 5: LEAD YOUR TEAMS THROUGH CHANGE

The world has been shrunk down to a screen. Be aware of new technologies and new skills you might need to learn and adopt. What skills might you need to have? In today's fast-paced landscape, social media has been taken over by AI, and Millennials are looking for autonomy and a balanced lifestyle. We can do more for them that will benefit the company. But if we stick with the old mentality and don't change with the times, we won't succeed. Becoming more innovative and creative will bring us more efficiency. We need a higher level of emotional intelligence, knowledge, and new technologies to stay relevant. We need to be quick to change to become more efficient for ourselves and our team.

STEP 6: BECOME A CUSTOMER EXPERIENCE EXPERT

Create a fun environment for your customers and your team. Observe your team overcoming objections, and ensure you have a guide for their response. Seek feedback and maintain a customer complaints program that facilitates immediate assistance, chain of command contact, quick resolution, and follow up.

STEP 7: DEVELOP A RISK-MANAGEMENT CULTURE

Always think of risk mitigation as the foundation of your business. In the same way you pour concrete to strengthen a house, risk mitigation is the foundation of your business. Follow company policy and procedures and make decisions accordingly. Furthermore, integrity is a key component of decision making. Always do the right thing, especially when no one is watching.

STEP 8: BECOME A PROFIT-DRIVEN LEADER

Your responsibility as a leader is to produce and help grow your company's bottom line by developing high-performing teams that execute effectively and meet the company's goals and objectives. It's okay to have a rough month, but that should be a one-off. You signed up to produce positive results. You were hired to make your team great, come up with innovative solutions, and own their goals. To reach your team's goals, create a plan that details who, what, where, and when. Use a calendar to manage your strategies, daily routine, and coaching culture. Have one-on-one sessions with each team member and talk about goals, gaps, strategies, action plans, best practices, etc.

STEP 9: BECOME RESPONSIBLE FOR YOUR OWN DEVELOPMENT

Through continuous education and awareness of where you are and where you want to go, develop a training plan. Work with your manager to get the resources to help you, but in the end, your development is up to you. You need to be vocal, immerse yourself in company culture, join diversity chapters, participate in seminars, and attend industry events. Remember, your voice matters. No one will give you a promotion without you first taking steps to become a leader. It's simply a way of thinking, acting, and taking steps toward success. Know you are ready to lead larger teams, make a difference in people's lives, and lead them to greatness to the company's benefit. You have many layers, and it's time to unleash them one by one and start your leadership journey.

Where a cohesive team lives, a positive atmosphere grows!

STEP 10: CREATE FUTURE LEADERS

Leaders create future leaders. To start creating the next leaders who will serve our beautiful nation, let's look at the action you need to take.

1. **Identify those on your team with leadership skills.** If they don't have leadership skills, find those with a strong desire to become leaders. That should be your motivator. Never dismiss someone with no skill who wants to become something big because they can—anyone can. Remember Jerry, the driven one? He didn't have many leadership skills, but he was willing to work hard and learn from me. In a few short years, Jerry became a financial advisor for one of the largest and most successful banks in existence. Today, he helps people manage their hard-earned money. In my opinion, you should encourage your entire team to move

to the next meaningful leadership role, but some people will be happy where they are and love what they do, and that's okay too.

2. **Foster a positive culture for learning.** Create a culture of care. Hold one-on-one development sessions where you sit each week, month, quarter, semi-annually, and annually. Identify actionable items for them to learn and grow, and keep them accountable. Ensure they do the work, and help them get there. Knowing the timeline and individual roadmap to reach their goals is critical for each aspiring leader. Following through is the most important piece to ensure continuing growth, so be sure to use your calendar and schedule times that work for both of you.

3. **Create mentorship across your organization.** You can't do everything on your own; you also have a business to run, so ensure you find a mentor for future leaders. It can be someone from your department or outside, so long as it is someone who is thriving and willing to teach. Talk to the mentors about your team members and what other resources they can provide. There might be leadership groups, organizations, or local chapters that they can join for additional help. If your aspiring leader joins these programs, ensure you have a discussion at each follow-up meeting to find out what they learned and what went well to show you care about their development.

4. **Provide feedback and recognition along the way.** Everyone wants feedback on how they are progressing along their learning path. Highlight their strengths and areas of opportunities. Ensure you give constructive feedback so it can help them grow and develop their skills. Recognize them for the great work they are doing; highlight the areas where they have achieved, whether a small or big accomplishment. Write a handwritten note about their milestone and their willingness to learn and grow. This will motivate them and inspire them because they will feel they are not alone but you are there holding their hand.

5. **Create opportunities and provide resources for leadership jobs.** Once your team member is ready to go to the next step in becoming a leader, ensure they know how to find the jobs and are getting ready to master the interview process. As a leader, I advise you to have patience

because this will be a step that might bring disappointments if they are not finding a leadership job. Prepare them by letting them know this is the last step, and it's a big step to prepare for the interview process. They need to be responsible for their own development as I talked about in Chapter 10. Help them with updating their resume, and ensure they update their qualifications. Have them write their bio. Let them start building their scenarios and have them write them as they come up with them. Keep practicing the SAR (situation, action, result) format. Keep practicing scenarios and common interview questions with them. If they have a fear of speaking in public or a fear of higher authority—and we all have these or other fears—work with them on their self-esteem and confidence. Use resources from Chapter 2 to help them build their champion mindset.

6. **Celebrate your future leader with your entire team.** When your aspiring leader becomes a leader and lands their job, hold a big celebration with your team. Celebrate the leader's new job and be very proud of yourself for getting another person to their desired destination. It's an amazing accomplishment; it's like you are birthing a baby. It's your baby, so be proud of what you have done for another individual and their family. Invite all the mentors, your new leader, and anyone who helped along the way. Let everyone celebrate a great moment in life—someone becoming a leader in this amazing world.

EXERCISE

1. Become more self-aware so you can grow. We are not aware of everything going on inside of us. Look inside to see how much you know, how much you want to learn, and if you have success blocks holding you back. Think about the following questions, write detailed answers, and be open to feedback. Seek feedback from peers or your manager once you've answered the questions below.

_____
_____
_____

2. How can I become more intentional and self-aware every day?

3. Where are my opportunities, and what are my success blocks?

4. Where am I strongest, and how can I continue to help others develop and grow?

> *"True leaders don't create followers; they create more leaders."*
> — J. Sakiya Sandifer

Imagine now what is about to happen. All your hard work and follow through have paid off, personally and professionally. You visualized your job, interviewed, and received a happy phone call.

Congratulations! Getting a leadership position is so rewarding. You are ready to lead larger teams—you deserve the promotion.

Now it's time to celebrate and continue your path to greatness. Remember the skills you need, including soft skills. Always be kind and wear your best smile. Approach decision-making by focusing on what's important to your company and your team, and lead your team to success. I really believe this formula is the mark of a great leader and will help you leave an everlasting legacy. You will be proud when someone you helped sees you at a restaurant one day and tells you that you helped them build a better life.

As a leader, remember you still work for your managers. You need to bring those managers to leadership too—one manager at a time.

STEP 10 - LEADERS CREATE FUTURE LEADERS

If you lead with your heart, empathy, compassion, and humility, and listen, coach, observe, and give timely feedback, you will be great at execution and on your way to endless opportunities. Remember, Rome was not built in a day. You are becoming a leader who will leave a positive mark. You are the *legacy leader*. Go help the world become a better place. I will be rooting for you because we are all in this world and connected in the most magical way. I believe in you and your ability to become great!

Developing others brings happiness, which brings me to my last chapter. I wrote it for the newcomer, the immigrant, the refugee, etc. Immigrants in the United States have moved here to live and make a life for themselves. Some came because a parent landed a job, others faced economic instability, and still others fled a war and came as refugees.

Regardless of the reason, they are here now, and they have been trying hard to adjust to a new culture. It's not an easy transition. If you only knew. I will try to shed as much light as I can on the experience in the next chapter, so together, we can help newcomers and make them feel welcomed, heard, valued, and accepted.

When my friend Jen read the chapter, as I made coffee, I heard her laugh out loud.

"What is so funny?" I asked.

"I love the America pie part," she said. "I need to be reading this too. Half of the things I don't do will help me too."

So, it would be an honor for me if you will share the next chapter with someone who is new here to help them. It was the most emotional chapter to write because it was me thirty years ago, and I wish then someone had told me the things I have written here.

The information will help newcomers to the United States expedite the process and adapt quickly. Please don't skip it. Check it out and share it. Let's go—we're almost there!

"Immigrants have always been a key part of the American success story. They have built and contributed to our economy, our communities, and our innovation. They embody the entrepreneurial spirit that fuels our nation's progress and have reached our society with diverse perspectives. We must continue to embrace and support immigrants, for they are a vital source of talent, creativity, and strength."
— Satya Nadella

CHAPTER 12: BONUS CHAPTER

ACCELERATING INTEGRATION FOR IMMIGRANT SUCCESS

"Our attitude towards immigration reflects our faith in the American ideal. We have always believed it possible for men and women who start at the bottom to rise as far as the talent and energy allow. Neither race nor place of birth should affect their chances."
— Senator Robert F. Kennedy

It was Christmas Day, 1987. I arrived in America with my younger brother and my mom. My father had already been working in America for five years and brought my older brother over two years after he got here. I was amazed when my father was driving us to the apartment in the New Jersey suburbs and asked, "Where are all the people?" No one was outside, but the streets were lit up with beautiful Christmas lights. *It is magical*, I thought, watching through the car window. I was overwhelmed with joy. I had arrived in America— I couldn't believe my eyes. My heart was pounding with excitement for what was yet to come. Finally, I had arrived in the most beautiful land of opportunity—opportunity for everyone, including me. Nowhere other than America do you get to taste this type of freedom. We should never take it for granted.

After twenty-five years working here professionally and traveling to many lands, I still say…the United States of America is the best country on the entire planet. We are free to be who we are, become whoever we want to be, with no one stopping us and telling us we can't do it. We can do it!

Waiting for my American citizenship took a while, but it was one of my proudest moments when I took an oath of allegiance at the naturalization ceremony. I cried my happy tears, and I was overwhelmed with joy when I was given my certificate of naturalization. My proof of US citizenship was in my hands, and I was so grateful, so blessed to be given the opportunity to serve this amazing country and be part of it. This incredible feeling has never left me—the feeling of receiving the greatest gift ever, and I kept repeating to myself, *I am an American citizen. I am an American citizen!* I felt I could fly. I could now travel the world and become whoever I wanted to be without judgment. My road was clear, and I knew success would come to me. What an honor it is to come from a small country and become a part of a big dream. My added oath was "I am in your debt, and I will only repay you with good, America," so I started.

I had big dreams when I got here, and I thought no matter what obstacle I had to face, I would deal with them and overcome them with hard work, critical thinking, determination, and love from my heart. I knew this migration helped my development, but it was not easy. My road consisted of so many twists, turns, and roadblocks. I didn't know my way back home, and my torn heart fought for years. For many days, I felt like I lived in a dark forest waiting for some light to come through, but I was young, in a new world, waiting for someone's smile to warm my day. I was learning the language, learning who I was, and going through the education process. If you came from a different country, I know your pain. We've shared the same difficult experiences yet have carried such love in our hearts for humanity and diversity, and we want to include and embrace the entire world.

Welcome to the most beautiful country in the world. Congratulations on your arrival. I am calling on you, my immigrant friend, to become a leader with empathy and compassion. No matter what profession you choose, everyone needs self-leadership skills to succeed. I feel what you are going through, your struggles. I have been there, and there is a light at the end of the tunnel—a bright light. Make sure you put your working hat on, and let's go!

If my body could speak, it would curse me for the negative self-talk, fear, insecurities, lack of self-love, lack of confidence, torment, and self-sabotage that took me decades to resolve in my own mind.

I am determined to help you, my immigrant friend. It's my mission, my calling to cut years off your struggle, torment, and self-sabotage and bring you to your blissful state—the state in which I live every day. I want to make every day your best day!

Below is an accelerated process for your development.

SIX ACTIONS FOR EARLY IMMIGRANT DEVELOPMENT IN SCHOOL OR WORK

ACTION 1: TRUST YOURSELF

Trust yourself, your unique talents and skills, and create your own roadmap to success. Draw a roadmap of where you are and where you want to go. For example, make one destination on your roadmap be to learn the language. Sign up for an English as a second language (ESL) course. In high school or college, learn the language while working to build the professional skills you need to succeed, such as communication, listening, diversity and inclusion, customer experience skills, etc.

Create your roadmap now, while you are at point A. How will you get to point B? Include resources, needed skills, and the timeframe for reaching your goal.

Remember, you are in the land of opportunity; there is no limit to what you can do—the sky is the limit!

ACTION 2: EMBRACE AMERICAN CULTURE

As a newcomer, it's hard to meet people, and the language barrier is a problem, but you have to push yourself, get out there, and communicate the best you can. Use body language, make it humorous, whatever works. You can't be shy due to limited English skills. Just come out of your shell and use what you know. Use technology. Use Google translator or any of the many apps to help you learn the art of communication here. The internet is full of information.

I wholeheartedly embraced everything about American culture—the food, history, museums, music, art, movies, and places to see. Go out and explore. Don't be confined to just your own people and culture. Make it a point to meet new people and tell them you are new here and you want to make friends. You will become well-versed and knowledgeable with time, and then you won't feel afraid of the unknown. American culture is beautiful, free of judgment, and loves knowing we are made of immigrants. America will embrace you and help you or simply be a good friend.

In American high school, I made many friends. I spent years celebrating friendships with them. In college, I joined student government to learn and meet people. I have spent a lot of time with those people over the years.

ACTION 3: LEARN ABOUT PEOPLE, AND CULTIVATE A DIVERSE CIRCLE OF FRIENDS

Along the way, you will meet Americans and many others. Every country, culture, and people has its own beauty, and everyone has unique traits and customs. Look at their stories with love. Different is beautiful. Be curious, and ask questions with enthusiasm and love. We all love to talk about our culture, hometown, food, dress, experiences, travel, etc.

When I was in ESL class, I tried to meet and learn about everyone in my class. We were a melting pot of Macedonians, Italians, Poles, Russians, etc. Everyone's unique perspective has its own beauty. Listen and learn about their ideas, make friends, go to their restaurants, and experience their cuisine, which is another way of learning about them. Always make it a point to learn about others—it's your learning time and you are a student in a new world of many possibilities.

I met my first friend, and now my best friend of thirty-five years, when I first arrived. Take friendships seriously—you never know how significant that friend may become. All it takes is love and an open heart.

Where can you meet these individuals and groups? The many options include school, places of worship, trusted groups on Facebook, or by creating your own group.

ACTION 4: FIND A MENTOR TO GUIDE YOU

It's important to find someone who can help you along the way, whether it is with your move here, your paperwork, your development, or your career goals. Regardless of which stage of your success journey you are in, seek help and have a mentor. Your mentor is someone you can connect with. They can be a school counselor, trusted advisor, cousin, friend, religious leader, virtual coach, etc. They are someone to walk with you on your journey and help you along the way while holding you accountable. Accountability is very important and keeps you working toward your goals. Meet with your mentor monthly to discuss your goals and accomplishments, and at the end of the conversation, discuss what you will work on during the following month and so on. I wish I had known what a mentor was and had one to guide me when I first came—it would have set me up for success much sooner. I wish you the best of luck.

ACTION 5: HAVE A LIMITLESS MINDSET AND EMBRACE ALL POSSIBILITIES

Work on your mindset and have a healthy daily routine. I wish someone had told me long ago that our subconscious believes what we tell it and we can fix our thought process. I have been in the self-development arena for many years, and I know from the past that schools, colleges, and work don't develop the skills you need to change your internal dialogue. Equip yourself to live a better life, wake up with joy, and laugh each day. No matter what the day brings, you can be in a blissful state knowing you will be okay. So be gentle with yourself, speak beautiful words to yourself, and have grace.

You left your home and perhaps your family behind for better opportunities and a better life for you and your loved ones. I know it can be heartbreaking, but think of the prosperous future full of endless opportunities awaiting you. Those opportunities will benefit your entire family. Please be patient. For me, after thirty-plus years in America, I still think about the beautiful lake where

I swam each day and the cafés where I sat and gazed at the most beautiful scenic views. I miss my neighborhood. Many of my friend's beautiful moms passed away, but I made sure they were all well taken care of when I visited. You will also make a significant change in other people's lives; just continue on the path of love and open your heart, following it when it speaks to you.

With love everything is possible, but the most important love is self-love—love yourself first so you can love others.

The steps to achieving a limitless mindset are:

- Think big! Trick your mind and visualize the success ahead as if it is already here.
- Write your future letter describing the future you and whom you will become.
- Write out your daily routine.
- Work on your mindset, changing it from negative to positive—how?
- Wake up with a plan and the intentions of having a positive day—intention is very important in whatever you do. It tells your mind what you will do.
- Pray to your Higher Power or what you believe in, or meditate and visualize—you can do one or all of these, depending on what you like to do. I do all of them or mix them up. You can find resources on my references page.

Daily affirmations are my favorite, and so easy to do. They are like seeds for the soul. You repeat phrases to yourself and affirm things to help you believe positive things. It is like reprogramming your mind. I have struggled with always doing for others and not for myself, giving too much, and loving too much. At times, it left me feeling rundown. I was a doer for my parents to ensure they were okay. When my younger brother got sick, I exhausted myself to the point I could hardly stand. Someone who knew me pointed out I needed self-love. By repeating phrases such as, "I am worthy. I love myself. I am my own best friend. I appreciate myself. I choose to be kind to myself," etc., I got back on track. That took me a month of daily thirty-minute sessions, so ensure you give yourself enough time to fix whatever area you want to fix.

Start your self-development and reach your full potential. You can heal any area and eliminate any limiting beliefs by following these steps. I will be rooting for you. Good luck!

ACTION 6: CELEBRATE YOUR MILESTONES, SUCCESSES, AND ACCOMPLISHMENTS

It is important to celebrate what you have worked on. Celebrate meeting a new friend, learning ten more words, or eating American cheesecake—any big or small moment can be worth celebrating. Incorporate celebration into your personal and professional journey because with celebration, gratitude, and appreciation, life is very motivating and happy—your heart will thank you. Invite others you meet along the way to celebrate with you. I wish I had celebrated small things, but instead, I was always waiting for big things. Now I celebrate myself daily—it can be as small as having a piece of dark chocolate, but I celebrate.

Travel, see things, and if you can (if you have your green card or citizenship), experience world travel. Traveling is one way to learn about diversity and expand your mind because you see different cultures and experience different foods, architecture, landscapes, and cultures within cultures.

For example, states have their signature foods. New York is proud of its New York style pizza, Pennsylvania is proud of its cheesesteak, and Texas is proud of its Tex-Mex cuisine. These are just a few of my favorites. Seeing Washington, DC is amazing and so historic. The beaches of Florida are beautiful, and Hollywood is a dream. I pinched myself when I was there. When you have a free weekend or vacation, it's important to plan what you want to see.

Keep in mind for the future that world travel is amazing. Visiting different continents, countries, cities, beaches, etc., seeing different lands, swimming in different oceans, and immersing yourself in different cultures, cuisines, and people is priceless. After becoming a citizen, I was so happy to experience many beautiful lands. I visited Rio de Janeiro during Carnival, Sydney in Australia, Capri and Venice in Italy, and many others. I had to wait until I was established and able to travel, which was difficult. But I got there, and you will too. What's on your bucket list? You have some traveling to do. Let's go!

RECAP

Draw your roadmap showing where you are now and what you want to become: find or create a process to go by, and remember you can do anything—so carve your own path to success.

My roadmap included embracing American culture and learning as much as I could. I made it a point to learn something weekly, keep a journal of accomplishments, and recap monthly to see how much I accomplished. Examples: meeting a new friend on a bus, singing the national anthem, or trying a piece of apple pie. I remember singing "Take Me Out to the Ballgame" with my Chinese friend in my ESL class, and we were laughing out loud about who could sing louder—such a fun memory. Please make it fun and exciting, and do it with a friend so you can look forward to it!

Week 1 Lessons

For example: Identify basic services in your community (buses, schools, hospitals, food markets, movie theaters) and learn basic English phrases, etc.

_____

_____

_____

Week 2 Lessons

For example: Explore American customs and traditions, overcoming culture shock, etc.

Week 3 Lessons

For example: Learn about legal matters and documentation (visas, green card) or about other immigration assistance programs, care programs.

Week 4 Lessons

For example: Financial literacy: opening a bank account and learning banking services, budgeting, and saving tips.

Recap Month

For example: What have you accomplished and learned so far?

Learn about people, and have a diverse circles of friends. At the beginning, when I came, I went to a small town full of Macedonians, and I hung out with them after school and on weekends. That did not serve me well. I was afraid of others at the time, and language was a problem for me, but I needed to push through that fear. No one told me how to live in a diverse world, but I knew I had to. Doing so is very important for your personal and professional growth—expand your circle and make it your strategy to build a diverse circle of friends.

Journal monthly about the people you met and how you have expanded your diverse circle.

Month 1: How many people have you met?

_____

_____

Month 2: How many people have you contacted and met for a cup of coffee?

_____

_____

Month 3: How many additional people have you met by now and where are they from?

_____

_____

Month 4: Have you started to form relationships, and do you have a diverse group yet?

_____

_____

And so on…

Find a mentor to guide you. Write to people or organizations you think have the potential to be your mentor and the ability to keep you accountable. If you are new and don't know anyone, google organizations in your town or go to the offices, nonprofit organizations with volunteers to help immigrants, schools, and/or colleges with programs for immigrants, or find internet associations that can work with you on Zoom, etc.

My mentor is:

_____

I meet with my mentor monthly or weekly:

_____

We discuss my mission and goals as follows:

_____

We discuss how will I get there by working on A, B, and C:

_____

We discuss my progress toward my goals:

_____

I am _____ percent of the way to my personal goals, which are:

_____

I am _____ percent of the way to my professional goals, which are:

_____

Traveling is amazing for the soul. You can immerse yourself in the culture, food, architecture, and landscape. Add an ongoing process to your schedule to spend free weekends or vacation time to travel. Set a long-term goal of world travel to expand your mind and promote diversity. Let's set a goal for traveling.

Travel calendar examples:
- Weekend in Boston
- Week's vacation at Clearwater Beach
- Which week-long destination within the USA works and when?
- Which weekend destination within USA works?
- What is your destination within the USA, month and place?
- Future world travel bucket list country and when?

HAVE A LIMITLESS MINDSET

Become unstoppable. Be sure of yourself, and love yourself. Don't think you have limitations on what you can do. If you fear internal limitations, and we all have them, write them down and start working on them.

External limitations might be the fear or belief that you won't be able to succeed in this country, you'll be rejected, you'll be unable to communicate or get your point across, you won't be able to change your perspective on the culture, etc.

I will overcome external limitations through prayer/affirmations/meditation/positive visualization:

day _____ time _____

day _____ time _____

Internal limitations might be the fear or belief that you can't get past unresolved issues, love yourself, or find your self-worth, or that you are undeserving of love, peace, prosperity, or you have a poverty mindset when it comes to money.

I will overcome internal limitations through prayer/affirmations/meditation/positive visualization:

day _____ time _____

day _____ time _____

Release your limitations and set yourself free. I am waiting for you on the other side, waiting for a whole you, the best version of you, the one who loves themselves and then loves others, the one who believes success can be earned with hard work, determination, and an open and positive mindset. Things won't be handed to you here, but by having a vision of where you want to go, being open to cultural differences and embracing them, making friends with anyone without judgment, and not being afraid of the unknown but respecting it, you will be setting yourself up for success.

Working with a mentor toward your future goals and celebrating your milestones, having fun and traveling the beautiful land of opportunity, and expanding when you can through world travel, you will become unstoppable on your way to your amazing future. It's waiting for you.

I love words. You can do magic with words, but only utter good ones to help people, and be silent when you can't find anything good to say. Don't hurt anyone—that's not your job. Only spread love!

Deep down, I always thought I was a poet. Once, as a child, I was sitting under the bridge when we had a once-a-year poetry night in Struga, Macedonia. Poets from all over the world were performing. It was so inspiring. It made me want to write. When I came to the USA, I didn't speak English, so it was hard for me to continue writing. I am glad I was able to keep my dream alive. It's never too late to revive a dream. I wrote the following poems, and they represent the stories of my life. I hope some resonate with you!

ARRIVING

I closed my eyes,

Driving down memory lane.

I remember no people, only rain

Where my home was when I first came.

It was Christmas Day.

Street was embellished.

Old apartment with dark wood floors,

Small place, wood furniture, and old doors.

I spent my days in tears.

Many sleepless nights, just glares.

Left my friends, my town, my lake.

A month passed, and I felt it was a mistake.

I started school, a new promise,

A glimpse of hope was slowly arising.

New friends and new beginnings.

Curiosity intrigued me, I started dreaming.

The smell of our new home made me happy.

My room was my haven where I studied.

College years were hard but rewarding.

Proud, I was ready for the onboarding.

THE STUDENT

Years of learning and studies and I did it!

Many sleepless nights, struggles but I beat it.

The language I learned word by word.

Repetition is key is what I've heard.

Running after my dream was halfway there.

Graduation was a milestone in the open air.

Waiting for loved ones but no one was near.

My friend's family embraced me and said not to fear.

I wiped my tears all alone.

Faced the celebration on my own.

The honor students and that was my name.

I looked up at the sky and thanked God for that day.

Did I feel the emptiness inside?

For years I struggled with why no one was by my side.

Decades passed and now I know,

Can't blame anyone for what they don't know.

God, you raised me with love all by your own.

You wiped my tears as I went along.

You instilled a powerful heart inside of me.

I live today with the strongest will.

SWEET CHILDHOOD

Many decades have passed in my life.

My sadness for the South still remains.

I remember the most joy and laughter,

The memories of my friends still stay.

I felt indulgence in my beautiful lake,

Endless days swimming to its shores.

The small poetic town filled with grace,

If I turn time, I will be again in that place.

Days we picked flowers in the valleys,

Embracing the sun, playing outside.

Many hours at coffee shops watching

People gathering, storytelling…

Healthy living, eating daily fresh foods.

Markets filled with old ladies selling fruits.

Singing in the chorus made me feel alive.

And a decade of gymnastics helped me thrive.

A December day filled with happiness.

Secretly brought me emptiness.

Going to a land where people dreamed of

Forgetting all that I left behind was unheard of.

HELLO, HOMELAND

Why hasn't this sun warmed my tiny bones?

My eyes haven't seen blue waters like yours,

Haven't felt the breeze the way I felt it there.

My longings for you were everywhere.

I have dreamed many dreams of your view,

Waited for years to come see you.

At last, immigrant status faded into dust.

My heart ached, filled with such a lust.

I arrived with a big smile, and I saw you.

Crowds of families anticipated for years

Release the emptiness and bring happy tears,

melting away with no more fears.

Walked the missed grounds for days.

I swam and faded into your sweet embrace.

Days filled with incredible memories.

You sang to me my sweetest harmony.

WELCOME TO YOUR BREATH

Contentment knocked on my door one day,

Whispered to me and said I am here to stay.

I am not a guest. I have waited for you.

From gratitude and prayer each day

happiness and joy came my way.

My enemy has lived here and never paid the rent.

What a pity, but no! It's never too late.

You looked far to find your treasure.

Decades have passed and you finally saw,

Far away love was always near.

The path you took that ended up astray

Brought you to the strong human today.

If you found it, you will not be so wise

To teach the world what's kind.

Your heart is!

THE CONSULTANT

Dad, I always said I will make you proud.

Worked until midnight and some more.

Communication and presentations galore!

Then the pandemic came upon us all.

Many sleepless nights, ups and downs.

My scars became my lessons.

At times with no comfort but had to be done.

Standing tall as I entered each time.

Years of racing against time

Wanting to excel in all my dreams.

And nothing could stop me.

Without fear, my integrity was near.

I put on my best suit and wore my smile.

Spoken like a true leader each time,

Led from my heart and left them speechless.

Now it's time to enjoy all my reaches.

And watch my leaders grow one by one!

MAGIC MOMENTS

Wake up early, see the sunrise in motion.

Say good morning and put on your favorite lotion.

Barefoot stand on the grass so green.

End with watching the moon kissing the ocean.

You are not broken; shake it off.

Thank your refrigerator for keeping your food cold.

Sing and dance to the music inside of you.

Smile at your stove cooking your stew.

Start creating your magical world.

Don't wait for others and never feel old.

Stop the endless storm inside you.

Find your treasure and never feel blue.

Look inside you!

HEARTFELT LOVE

One day, when I die, if they asked me,

"What one thing do you love the most?"

I will say, "It's my beautiful son, Sammy."

My baby boy, you, my darling you!

I will stay as long as I can to be with you.

To be your strong support and your go-to.

When you are about to fall, I will catch you.

When you get sick, my love will heal you.

Never felt love as deep and as pure.

Your love for me was my mental cure.

I kept going during times when I was weak.

For a boy named "All-Hearing" and so unique!

My life, my angel, my longings

Even when you are near, I still miss you.

Love like this, I never thought I would find.

A miracle of God and one of a kind.

May you find this special love!

TRUE FRIEND

I found you when my days were gray.

I build a mountain of gratitude every day.

'Til my last breath, I want you to stay.

Without you, I won't live another day.

We are connected by an invisible thread.

Even if it breaks, it connects again.

For you, my friend, I always pray,

For your sweet son to find the best way.

Your presence gives me so much strength.

If I need you, you never lead me astray.

You have a heart like no other.

Great friend, a sister, and a great mother!

Sending love through my eyes to you!

I hope you like my poems. These poems are about my journey since I came to America. I wrote them last year when I was ready to write my poetry book, but our lives took a different turn. It was unfortunate that my dearest younger brother, Baskim, was diagnosed with stage-four lung cancer, and I couldn't concentrate on my poetry. But I wanted him to be excited about something, so I asked him if he would allow me to write about his journey and his positive beliefs to help people accept, adapt, and live with cancer. Excited, he agreed, and we started on the project with the help of a book coach.

We offered forty loving suggestions for coping with cancer or anything difficult. The book was published, and it is a beautiful memorial to my late brother. He passed five days after the book was published, but he held it in his hands, and his legacy and positivity will live forever.

I tell you this because life is full of unexpected turns. If someone told me today if we hadn't moved to the United States, Baskim would be alive, I would not care about any of my success. Losing a sibling is like losing a limb—you will never be the same again.

Be kind and loving to your siblings and family, create only happy memories, and resolve any issues. Nothing is worth holding onto because one day we are here, and the next day we might not be. Be well!

"The function of leadership is to produce more leaders and not followers."
— Ralph Nader

A FINAL NOTE

"Leadership is a skill that can be learned, for as long as you have a conscious learning plan towards it."
— Yukti Kapoor Mehandiratta

Dear Reader,

As this book comes to an end, I want to repeat and sum up the processes herein so you can remember the ten solutions to your success—we all learn by repetition.

I wrote this book while grieving my younger brother's passing. I spent seventy-two days in the hospital, mostly in the ICU, by my brother's side, and I still have flashes of heartbreaking scenes. But I am so grateful I helped him at the hardest time of his life. I recently published an article about how I overcame my grief that I hope will help others cope with theirs. The article talked about the same processes we looked at in Chapter 2: Building your Champion Mindset, that also helped me heal. It's all in our mindset.

Our failures and our successes lie in our mindset. I tell you this so you can release any trauma inside you. I have gone through a traumatic event, but I choose to continue living and fixing myself every day so I live a better life full of purpose. I have a family to take care of, a child to raise.

Always be your authentic self and speak from your heart. Do you know how nervous I used to get when I had to speak to leadership when I was a manager? My heart raced so badly that I thought I was going to faint. Nothing is worth that stress. Say what you have to say in your own way. Be your authentic self. Let your voice be heard, and don't worry about someone's vocabulary being better than yours. Let your words reflect your heart. You will succeed faster because people will look up to you and trust you.

Who thought I would be writing a leadership book? I always wanted to write a book, but one about being a "victim of culture," as I thought I was. Later, I realized I wasn't a victim of my own culture; my culture is beautiful, but I was mad at people who didn't know any better. After I realized this and released all the limitations, I was no longer a prisoner in my own skin. I was destined for greatness. Why am I telling you all this? Because I don't want you to hold on to childhood or family drama or hold grudges against anyone. You and your health are all you need to nurture and the most important gift you will ever get.

Get up and dust yourself off. Start living. Speak from your heart and wear a smile. You'll brighten someone's day. Build your team one by one, day after day, with a plan and patience. Have courage. It's like building a house brick by brick. Create the same kind of blueprint for your development. "I am here today, and I want to be here in six months interviewing for a leadership position." Embrace diversity wholeheartedly and love people for whoever they are—we are all humans with the same organs, senses, feelings, and emotions. Include everyone. Use your influence and keep perfecting this skill. Learn how to be exceptional at dealing with change. It will help you successfully communicate change to your team.

Speak positive words full of wisdom and understanding. Embrace your team and your customers and build long-term, loyal relationships. Be an expert in risk management and ensure everyone does things right the first time. This will build trust among your customers, and they will come back to do business with you. Become a revenue expert and dive deep into product development. Know your business, innovate when opportunities present themselves, and turn them into successes. Become responsible for your own development, create your vision board, and use your calendar—honor your time with your activities. Become the leader you always wanted to be, and help others follow in your footsteps. Become a *Legacy Leader* who creates future leaders and leaves a mark on this world that reflects all your great deeds. When you leave this world, what is left behind is your legacy. Be the leader today whom others will follow tomorrow.

I wish you all the best on your road to *Becoming a Legacy Leader.*

In conclusion, I would personally like to thank you for purchasing and investing your time in reading this book. Please share it with your friends and family, or purchase it for a loved one you think will benefit from it.

Your input is very valuable. If you found this book valuable, please leave me a helpful review on Amazon, letting me and others know what you thought about it.

I'm praying for your success and that you live life like a true legacy leader!

As a token of my gratitude, here is a daily affirmation to bring you success on your road to becoming a legacy leader. I invite you to use these affirmations for twenty-one days to create change within yourself.

I Am a Legacy Leader

I have wings to fly.

I communicate from the heart.

I have a daily routine.

I have no success blocks.

I do meditation.

I recite affirmations.

I visualize my great life.

I believe in prayer.

I have many skills.

I identify problems.

I find solutions.

I give without expecting anything in return.

I teach only kindness.

I coach with intention.

I inspire greatness.

I give autonomy to innovate.

I love without limits.

I have empathy.

I have compassion.

I am a legacy leader,

Spreading seeds of knowledge

And developing future leaders,

And walking through life with pure intention

And pure sincerity.

I love my life.

I love me.

I am enough.

— Zana Kenjar

ACKNOWLEDGMENTS

All praise and thanks to God.

My deepest gratitude goes to all the amazing people who brought my book to life: my awesome business and breakthrough coach, Christine Gail; my brilliant editors, Tyler Tichelaar and Larry Alexander of Superior Book Productions; and my creative designer Shiloh Schroeder of Fusion Works; and my publisher, Aviva Publishing of New York and the amazing Susan Friedmann. My gratitude also goes to my resilient writing coach, Daniel Hagadorn, and my amazing fellow writers who held me accountable: Tracy Irons, Pamela George, Brigita McInvale, Donna Herbel, Cynthia McQuade, and Cindy Sheridan. Thank you for all the testimonials. I truly appreciate you.

Special thanks to my late brother in heaven. Through pain and loss, I have created my leadership book, a legacy and a guide for my son Sammy and future leaders. Thanks also to my dear friends and mastermind communities for their love, support, and belief in my work.

I would like to convey my sincere gratitude to my family. You are my heart. Thank you for your patience and for rooting for me along the way!

REFERENCES

CHAPTER 1: LEARNING THE POWER OF THE LEGACY LEADER

Gallup website: www.gallup.com/workplace

Doherty, Sharon. "Leading with Empathy in Today's Working World." Forbes. April 7, 2022.

Gail, Christine. *Unleash Your Rising: Lead With Intention and Ignite Your Story.* Lake Placid, NY: Aviva Publishing, 2018.

CHAPTER 2: BUILDING YOUR CHAMPION MINDSET

"A simple, fast way to reduce stress." Mayo staff. mayoclinic.org

Dispenza, Joe. "10 Affirmations for Positive Thinking." YouTube. https://www.youtube.com/watch?v=S3M-bdvm53A

Dispenza, Joe. "20-Minute Powerful Guided Meditation." https://www.youtube.com/watch?v=j_a1IwXmeRQ

Hay, Louise. "11-Hour Sleep Meditation + Affirmations." https://youtu.be/LkpQ7OVFY5Q

Hay, Louise. *Heal Your Life.* https://youtu.be/z08nPlFYzxY

Hay, Louise. "Love Yourself Meditation." YouTube. https://youtu.be/XrHY34YytM0

Hussey, Matthew. "Transform Your Relationship." YouTube. https://www.youtube.com/watch?v=MOGME2sDgr8

Johnson, Dave. "Apple CEO Tim Cook wakes up every day at 3:45 a.m. I tried doing it for a week, and it made me shockingly productive." Businessinsider.com. August 28, 2019. https://www.businessinsider.com/tim-cook-wake-up-morning-routine-productivity-2019-8

Lakhiani, Vishen. "The 6-Phase Guided Meditation: 10-Minute Guided Meditation." You Tube. https://www.youtube.com/watch?v=etNjyLcsgJE

Peer, Marisa. "I Am Enough Guided Meditation." YouTube. https://www.youtube.com/watch?v=IX5m9FlZNrk

Peer, Marisa. "Guided Meditation for Physical Healing (Heal Your Body Today)," https://www.youtube.com/watch?v=uOy3ImZnXKY

Robbins, Tony. "Priming: The Daily Habit Tony Robbins Uses to Boost His Brain." YouTube. https://www.youtube.com/watch?v=faTGTgid8Uc

CHAPTER 6: LEADING YOUR TEAMS THROUGH CHANGE

Maxwell, John C. The 21 Irrefutable Laws of Leadership.

Maxwell, John C. *Developing the Leader Within You.*

CHAPTER 7: BECOMING A CUSTOMER EXPERIENCE EXPERT

Mitchell, Jack. *Hug Your Customer.*

CHAPTER 10: BECOMING RESPONSIBLE FOR YOUR OWN DEVELOPMENT

Falcon, Michael. "Responsible for Their Own Development." LinkedIn. May 28, 2014. https://www.linkedin.com/pulse/20140529000522-41048409-employees-need-to-be-responsible-for-their-own-development/

REFERENCES

CHAPTER 11: LEADERS CREATE FUTURE LEADERS

Richards, Jay. "5 Things to Look for in Your Future Leaders." Industry Week. February 7, 2023. https://www.industryweek.com/leadership/corporate-culture/article/21259656/5-things-to-look-for-in-your-future-leaders

CHAPTER 12: ACCELERATING INTEGRATION FOR IMMIGRANT SUCCESS

The International Institutes. "A National Movement of Resettlement and Inclusion." Available at https://www.iistl.org/wp-content/uploads/sites/5/2019/05/nathistorybooklet.pdf.

Popular free translation apps:

- Google Translate
- Microsoft Translator

Websites for non-profit organizations that provide educational resources and programs:

- International Institute of New England (IINE): https://iine.org/
- International Rescue Committee (IRC): https://www.rescue.org/
- United We Dream: https://unitedwedream.org/

Other Free Resources for Free Services:

- Pro bono legal services can include assistance with immigration paperwork, asylum applications, and other immigration-related legal matters.
- Public Libraries
- International Rescue Committee (IRC)
- Citizenship and Immigration Services (USCIS)

ABOUT THE AUTHOR

Zana Kenjar is a leader and writer with more than two decades of experience in developing future leaders. She has overcome many obstacles to achieve success. Born in Yugoslavia (today the Republic of North Macedonia), she migrated to the United States with her family at the age of sixteen. After graduating with a bachelor's degree in management science from Kean University, she began her career in retail. After transitioning to the banking sector, where she worked for seventeen years, she managed diverse teams and brought bank branches to success. She was promoted several times. In her last role as a regional senior risk consultant, she led larger teams, worked with senior leaders and business partners, and made a profound impact on the organization.

During the COVID-19 pandemic and the downsizing of the large bank, Zana was displaced from her leadership job. At the same time, her younger brother was battling stage-four lung cancer. She helped her brother during the hardest time of his life, and it prompted her to write a book about his journey to share his positive beliefs. *In Search for the Miraculous Cure* offers forty loving suggestions for those affected by cancer or anything difficult. After her brother passed away in July 2022, Zana quickly landed a writing job. Today she has a blog where she writes poetry and business articles. She is currently writing a novel with two international writers.

In addition, Zana has pivoted from corporate work to creating her own path to success. During her time of grief, she felt compelled to write *Becoming a Legacy Leader*. She poured into it everything she knew about successful leadership to help the world and create amazing future leaders. She also began her leadership consulting business to help leaders and organizations thrive.

Zana is a caring, motivated, and selfless leader who is passionate about personal development and helping others. Her goal is to help as many people as possible through her books and as an independent leadership consultant. She is a true example of resilience and determination. Her story is an inspiration to many and a reminder that no matter how difficult the situation is, it can be overcome, and you can succeed.

Zana has a large extended family with whom she spends a lot of her time. She is teaching her seven-year-old son Sammy how to become a great human and be strong academically. She recently celebrated launching his first children's book, *Sammy the Singing Carrot*, a story about the wonders of nature and the beauty of true friendship.

Zana loves world travel, spending time outdoors, swimming, and entertaining. She is a strong advocate of daily routines, prayer, meditation, visualization, and exercise. She believes life should never be taken for granted—every sunrise is a gift from God, a second chance, and it should never be wasted. Zana finds joy in helping others, especially those in need. Her desire to make the world a better place, to give without return beyond God's blessings, is her inspiration.

HIRE ZANA KANJAR TO SPEAK OR TEACH AT YOUR NEXT EVENT

Zana hopes you found what you needed from this book. If you want to take a deeper dive and explore further with Zana, she would love to help you solve your particular problems through additional services that she offers.

Does your organization need more from its managers and leaders? Do you feel like some are stuck rather than growing, some are unmotivated and need refinement, and some are not using the right tools and strategies to help their teams develop? As Founder and CEO of ZK Leadership Learning, Zana specializes in helping businesses of all sorts and sizes.

For organizations and teams, Zana is available for:

- One-on-one consulting
- Group coaching
- Leadership training
- Leadership workshops
- Twelve courses, each based on a chapter of *Becoming a Legacy Leader*
- Leadership Retreats

Zana Kenjar delivers leaders, businesses, and organizations, powerful strategies, customized solutions, and practical tools to ignite the leader within and achieve greater progress and success toward their vision.

Zana is well known for her charismatic, fun personality that creates magic in people's hearts, and she teaches organizations how to do the same through workshops, events, training, and speeches. Hire Zana to bring fun, greatness, and limitless potential to your leaders by instilling a champion mindset in them.

To find out how Zana can help you, contact her at:

www.ZanaKenjar.com

www.BecomingALegacyLeader.com

Contact Zana:

To stay informed of future leadership development and updates, you can also subscribe to Zana's social media:

LinkedIn: ZK Leadership

Facebook: Zana Kenjar Author

Instagram: Zana Kenjar Author

Twitter: Zana Kenjar Author

TikTok: ZK_Leadership

YouTube Channel: Zana Kenjar Author

PURCHASE BULK COPIES OF
BECOMING A LEGACY LEADER

Now you can share the magic of *Becoming a Legacy Leader* with your entire organization. Then you can help your leaders become true legacy leaders and attract limitless success while experiencing a balanced and joyful life.

Zana offers special rates for ordering copies of her book in bulk. To learn more, contact her at:

www.BecomingALegacyLeader.com

ENHANCING THE IMMIGRANT EXPERIENCE

As a former immigrant, Zana has navigated through all the difficulties of migration, overcoming many obstacles and achieving success to become who she is today. Hire Zana to help your employees, friends, and family who are immigrants, former immigrants, and ESL students to find their voice, accelerate their integration into this country, jumpstart their careers, release their fears, and become great leaders who live a fulfilling life in the United States.

Zana can help immigrants solve their problems through:

- Workshops
- Immigrant Experience Speeches and Stories
- Training
- Group Coaching
- One-on-One Coaching

Contact Zana at:

www.BecomingALegacyLeader.com

Made in the USA
Las Vegas, NV
14 December 2023